DRAMATISTS PLAY SERVICE

OUTSTANDING WOMEN'S MONOLOGUES

VOLUME TWO

Edited by CRAIG POSPISIL
with DANNA CALL

★

DRAMATISTS
PLAY SERVICE
INC.

OUTSTANDING WOMEN'S MONOLOGUES: VOLUME TWO
Copyright © 2010, Dramatists Play Service, Inc.

All Rights Reserved

INTRODUCTION

Several years ago I found myself in a theater bookstore looking at the large selection of monologue books. There were collections of all different stripes: comic monologues, dramatic monologues; monologues by women, by men; monologues collected by year; and many more. What caught my attention was that all of the collections included monologues from plays published by Dramatists Play Service where I work, and I thought, "Why not put together a monologue collection drawn solely from our plays?"

After all, Dramatists represents most of today's best playwrights, both exciting new authors just coming onto the scene, and well-established ones. We publish 41 plays that have won the Pulitzer Prize for Best Play and 27 that have won the Tony Award for Best Play.

So, I set about editing two collections of monologues from our recent plays, and *Outstanding Men's* and *Outstanding Women's Monologues* was born. Both collections were well received and quickly ran through their print runs. Now, with the invaluable editorial help and input of Danna Call, the series continues with *Outstanding Men's* and *Outstanding Women's Monologues: Volume Two.*

Each of these two new volumes contains over 50 monologues that we've selected from some of the exceptional plays published by Dramatists in the last several years. You'll find an enormous range of voices and subject matter, characters from their teens to their 60s, and authors of widely varied styles but all immensely talented.

Danna and I would particularly like to thank Diana Bedoya and Emily Kadish for their help in bringing these books to print.

We hope this new collection will be useful to you in finding new audition material, classroom work or just for the pleasure of reading. Perhaps you'll be introduced to some new authors as well. We know that you will find some very exciting writing for the theater in these pages.

Craig Pospisil
New York City

CONTENTS

ALMOST BLUE *by Keith Reddin* 7

ALMOST, MAINE *by John Cariani* 8

AMPHIBIANS *by Billy Roche* 10

THE ARCHITECTURE OF LOSS *by Julia Cho* 11

AUGUST: OSAGE COUNTY *by Tracy Letts* 14

AUGUST: OSAGE COUNTY *by Tracy Letts* 17

BE AGGRESSIVE *by Annie Weisman* 19

BEAUTIFUL CHILD *by Nicky Silver* 21

BEAUTY ON THE VINE *by Zak Berkman* 23

BHUTAN *by Daisy Foote* 24

A BICYCLE COUNTRY *by Nilo Cruz* 26

BLACK SHEEP *by Lee Blessing* 28

THE BOOK OF LIZ *by Amy Sedaris and David Sedaris* 29

CAROL MULRONEY *by Stephen Belber* 31

CAVEDWELLER *by Kate Moira Ryan, based on the novel by*
   Dorothy Allison 33

DEN OF THIEVES *by Stephen Adly Guirgis* 35

THE DIXIE SWIM CLUB
   by Jessie Jones, Nicholas Hope, Jamie Wooten 37

EVERYTHING WILL BE DIFFERENT *by Mark Schultz* 39

FABULATION OR, THE RE-EDUCATION OF UNDINE
   by Lynn Nottage 41

FLESH AND BLOOD *by Peter Gaitens, adapted from the novel by*
   Michael Cunningham 43

FROZEN *by Bryony Lavery* 45

THE GOAT OR, WHO IS SYLVIA? *by Edward Albee* 48

GOOD THING *by Jessica Goldberg* 50

GULF VIEW DRIVE *by Arlene Hutton* 51

HOLD PLEASE *by Annie Weisman* 53

INTIMATE APPAREL *by Lynn Nottage* 55

LAST OF THE BOYS *by Steven Dietz* *57*

LOVE-LIES-BLEEDING *by Don DeLillo* *59*

LOVE SONG *by John Kolvenbach* *61*

MARIE ANTOINETTE: THE COLOR OF FLESH
    by Joel Gross *63*

MISS WITHERSPOON *by Christopher Durang* *65*

MONTHS ON END *by Craig Pospisil* *68*

THE MOONLIGHT ROOM *by Tristine Skyler* *71*

A MOTHER'S LOVE from LIFE IS SHORT *by Craig Pospisil* *72*

THE O'CONNER GIRLS *by Katie Forgette* *74*

THE PAIN AND THE ITCH *by Bruce Norris* *76*

PRAYING FOR RAIN *by Robert Lewis Vaughan* *78*

PYRETOWN *by John Belluso* *79*

THE RADIANT ABYSS *by Angus MacLachlan* *81*

REGRETS ONLY *by Paul Rudnick* *82*

A SMALL, MELODRAMATIC STORY *by Stephen Belber* *84*

SOUTHERN HOSPITALITY
    by Jessie Jones, Nicholas Hope, Jamie Wooten *86*

STRING FEVER *by Jacquelyn Reingold* *88*

THE STORY *by Tracey Scott Wilson* *90*

SUCH A BEAUTIFUL VOICE IS SAYEDA'S *by Yussef El Guindi,*
    adapted from the short stories by Salwa Bakr *92*

TEA *by Velina Hasu Houston* *94*

TEA *by Velina Hasu Houston* *95*

tempODYSSEY *by Dan Dietz* *97*

THIRD *by Wendy Wasserstein* *99*

TWO SISTERS AND A PIANO *by Nilo Cruz* *101*

WHITE PEOPLE *by J.T. Rogers* *103*

THE WIND CRIES MARY *by Philip Kan Gotanda* *105*

ALMOST BLUE

BY KEITH REDDIN

LIZ — 20s/30s.

SYNOPSIS: ALMOST BLUE is a stage noir set in a seedy rooming house, whose tenants include a man just out of prison trying to stay straight, a strange loner down the hall who writes pornographic greeting cards, a violent ex-con who wants to settle old scores and, of course, a beautiful woman in trouble who messes with everybody's head. Written in a series of brutal, funny encounters, ALMOST BLUE is a journey into the dark night, full of plot twists and sultry exchanges.

(Night. Liz and Phil in bed. Liz sitting up.)

LIZ. I used to think I would travel the world. Africa. China. Go to the movies, see these exotic places.

Some point though, you realize you're not going anywhere.

Once a year maybe you go to the city, take the train in, go to some bars, try to get in some club; they tell you to fuck off, you watch people getting out of their limos, beautiful people in beautiful clothes, they glide by, they glide right by you, they float, right into the club, the music pounding behind the door, and you're standing on the sidewalk watching them, watching them standing in the cold in some coat you got for Christmas three years ago, fucking freezing, watching the beautiful people, and you're stoned or drunk and it's raining and you're trying to pretend you're having a good time, trying to laugh and pretend this is special, but you're just fucking cold, it could be anywhere, but it's the city so it's great, so fucking great and you take the last train home, full of smoke and piss, somebody throwing up between cars, ice on the windows, it's two-thirty in the morning, you got to be at work in six hours, you look at your reflection and think this is it, this is my life.

But I know something. Not me. I'm gonna …

I'm getting the fuck away. Whatever it takes. I'm gonna get the fuck away, I don't know how, I just have to, I have to …

ALMOST, MAINE

BY JOHN CARIANI

HOPE — Who has traveled the world.

SYNOPSIS: On a cold, clear, moonless night in the middle of winter, all is not quite what it seems in the remote, mythical town of Almost, Maine. As the northern lights hover in the star-filled sky above, Almost's residents find themselves falling in and out of love in unexpected and often hilarious ways. Knees are bruised. Hearts are broken. But the bruises heal, and the hearts mend — almost — in this delightful midwinter night's dream.

WOMAN. *(Fast and furious; so absorbed by what she has to say and by what she has come to do, that she really doesn't take in/look at the man.)* I know this isn't going to be very easy, but I was just out there all alone in the world, and I got so scared, because all I could think about was how I had no place in this world, but then I just outta nowhere realized that there was one place in this world that I did have, and that was with you, so I flew and I took a taxi to get to you, I just had to come see you, *(Finally really looking at him.)* thank God you're — ... *(The man is not who she thought he'd be.)* Oh — ... Wait — ... I'm sorry. You're not — ... I'm — ... *(Checking to make sure she's at the right place.)* This is the house — ... I'm so sorry — ... Does Daniel Harding live here? I'm looking for Daniel Harding.
[MAN. You're // looking for —]
WOMAN. Looking for Daniel Harding, yeah. He *lives* here. I thought. But ... *(Off the man's confused state, realizing.)* ... ooooh ... he doesn't, does he? Oooh. I am so sorry. *(The woman gathers her bags, preparing to leave.)* I'm so embarrassed. "Who is this woman and what is she doing here?" *(Beat.)* I just honestly thought he'd be here. I always thought he'd be here. Always. *(Beat.)* Do you know him? Big guy, big tall guy. Played basketball, all-Eastern Maine, center? *Strong.* Do you know him? Played hockey, too?
[MAN. Well ... —]
WOMAN. Oh, don't even answer that. That was — . I know that's

a horrible question to ask a person who lives in a small town, as if everybody in small towns knows everybody else, agh!, can't believe I asked that. I don't live here anymore, but when I did, I hated it when people assumed I knew everybody in town just because it was small. It was worse than when they'd ask if we had " … plumbing way up there?," 'cause, you know, people in small towns really don't know each other any better than in big towns, you know that? I mean, you know who you know, and you don't know who you don't know, just like anywhere else. *(Beat.)* I'm so sorry to have bothered you. I was just so sure — . When his parents passed away, he kept the house, I heard. He lived here. He stayed here, I thought. He was one of the ones who stayed. *(Beat.)* I didn't stay. I went away.

AMPHIBIANS

BY BILLY ROCHE

BRIDIE — 30s.

SYNOPSIS: AMPHIBIANS is a dark, elegiac tale of the sea. Eagle, the last fisherman on the river, is about to give up the ghost and go to work in the soulless Menapia Seafood Plant. Before he does, though, he decides to unearth a long-dead ritual: to bring his ten-year-old son, symbolically named Isaac, out to Useless Island and leave him there alone in a solitary rite of passage. This act sparks off a fire beneath the cauldron of scorn, envy, resentment and plain heartache that has been festering all around him, which ends in a blistering climax of violence.

PLACE: Wexford, a small town in Ireland.

TIME: The present.

BRIDIE. You are a good lookin' fella, yeh know. Yeh remind me of a boy I used to know one time. He was a bit wild, too and all mixed up on the inside just like you are now. But unfortunately, he was just about to get married to someone else, when it all began. For three solid weeks, I met him every night behind Menapia Mansion there — under the Rose! It was probably just a last wild fling as far as he was concerned, but I fell hook, line and sinker for him. I swear I've never met anyone like him before or since. And God knows I've looked … I never told anyone about it. I never let the cat out of the bag on him. I don't think he even realised I was in trouble to tell you the truth. Well, if he did he never acknowledged it, anyway, let's put it that way. It was a baby boy — we buried him in a little overgrown grave with a wooden cross to mark the spot. Me Da painted the child's name on it but the rain came that night and washed it away … If he had've lived he would have been thirteen tomorrow — the tenth of November, St Martin's Eve — and I'd be singin' a different song today than the one I'm singin' now. Let her go, Zak. I know it's hard but sometimes when yeh love someone yeh just have to let them go.

THE ARCHITECTURE OF LOSS

BY JULIA CHO

CATHERINE — Greg's ex-wife. Very little affects her anymore. Mid-40s.

SYNOPSIS: It's another hot day in Tucson when a strange man arrives at Catherine's door. To her shock, he turns out to be Greg, her former husband who, sixteen years earlier, left and simply never came back. Now he has returned, but the family he left no longer exists. Catherine informs him that their son, David, disappeared eight years ago and remains missing. One by one each member of the family tells Greg a version of what happened that summer. Their stories are a meditation on loss, but they are also about the need for explanations, answers and, perhaps above all, absolution. For as they reveal their stories, the only thing that becomes clear is that the nine-year-old boy who vanished is far from the only thing they lost.

PLACE: On the outskirts of Tucson, Arizona.

TIME: Late summer.

CATHERINE. And he did.
    He got out. He got his things
    and walked right out the door.
    I stood right here and watched him.
    And then I turned around and saw David.
    I remember he was holding a basketball
    and what he did was,
    he hurled that ball
    right at my face as hard as he could.
    And then he ran out the door calling
    and calling after his grandfather …
    Just calling and calling his name.
    Dad didn't stop.

11

He didn't even turn around.
And David … he didn't come back inside.
I thought … well, I thought he just needed
to cool off a little. A short walk around
the neighborhood … do him some good.
It was four P.M. Daylight.
Nothing unusual about the day at all.
I think … I was folding laundry.
I'd like to say when it happened,
I felt something, like a tremor in the air. *(Lights shift.)*
(Calling.) David? Where are you?
David?
David? *(Beat.)*
But I didn't.
I didn't know anything at all.
[*GREG. You mean that was it?*
CATHERINE. No trace of him. No sign of him since.
GREG. But he's out there. There must be some clue, some lead —
CATHERINE. Nothing, there's nothing.
GREG. Let me talk to them, let me help —
CATHERINE. Greg. They've moved on to other cases. Other children.
GREG. Moved on? How can they do that, they can't do that.
CATHERINE. Of course they can.
GREG. But maybe I can —]
CATHERINE. Let me tell you something.
A boy and a man disappear. For a day.
At the end of that day, who walks back in
through the door? That's life for you.
The wrong ones get taken.
And they get taken all the time.
My father needs to be bathed. I do this.
He needs to be fed. I do this.
Every day, he becomes
more and more like an infant.
And my son, who every day
becomes more and more like a man,
he is somewhere I can't go.
He is someplace I can't reach.
We're taught that suffering is rewarded.
Suffer now and someday you will have

an equal share of happiness.
Well, I think this is bullshit.
I no longer believe in redemption.
I believe in suffering
without reason or reward.

AUGUST: OSAGE COUNTY

BY TRACY LETTS

KAREN WESTON: Bev and Violet's daughter, 40 years old.

SYNOPSIS: A vanished father. A pill-popping mother. Three sisters harboring shady little secrets. When the large Weston family unexpectedly reunites after dad disappears, their Oklahoman family homestead explodes in a maelstrom of repressed truths and unsettling secrets. Mix in Violet, the drugged-up, scathingly acidic matriarch, and you've got an unflinching — and uproariously funny — portrait of the dark side of the Midwestern American family.

PLACE: A large country home outside Pawhuska, Oklahoma, sixty miles northwest of Tulsa.

TIME: August 2007.

KAREN.   The present. Today, here and now. I think I spent so much of my early life thinking about what's to come, y'know, who would I marry, would he be a lawyer or a football player, would he be dark-haired and good-looking and broad-shouldered. I spent a lot of time in that bedroom upstairs pretending my pillow was my husband and I'd ask him about his day at work and what was happening at the office, and did he like the dinner I made for him and where were we going to vacation that winter and he'd surprise me with tickets to Belize and we'd kiss — I mean I'd kiss my pillow, make out with my pillow, and then I'd tell him I'd been to the doctor that day and I'd found out I was pregnant. I know how pathetic all that sounds now, but it was innocent enough ... Then real life takes over because it always does —
[BARBARA.   — uh-huh —]
KAREN.   — and things work out differently than you'd planned. That pillow was a better husband than any real man I'd ever met; this parade of men fails to live up to your expectations, all of them

14

so much less than Daddy or Bill (you know I always envied you finding Bill). And you punish yourself, tell yourself it's your fault you can't find a good one, you've only deluded yourself into thinking they're better than they are. I don't know how well you remember Andrew ...

[BARBARA. No, I remember.]

KAREN. That's the best example: Here's a guy I loved so intensely, and all the things he did wrong were just opportunities for me to make things right. So if he cheated on me or he called me a cunt, I'd think to myself, "No, you love him, you love him forever, and here's an opportunity to make an adjustment in the way you view the world." And I can't say when the precise moment was that I looked in the mirror and said, "Okay, moron," and walked out, but it kicked off this whole period of reflection, just swamped in this sticky recollection. How had I screwed it up, where'd I go wrong, and before you know it you can't move forward, you're just suspended there, you can't move forward because you can't stop thinking backward, I mean, you know ... years! Years of punishment, self-loathing. And that's when I got into all those books and discussion groups —

[BARBARA. And Scientology, too, right, or something like that? —]

KAREN. Yes, exactly, and finally one day, I threw it all out, I just said, "No, it's *me*. It's just *me*, here and now, with my music on the stereo and my glass of wine and Bloomers my cat, and I don't need anything else, I can live my life with myself." And I got my license, threw myself into my work, sold a lot of houses, and that's when I met Steve. That's how it happens, of course, you only really find it when you're not looking for it, suddenly you turn around and there it is. And then the things you thought were so important aren't really important. I mean, when I made out with my pillow, I never imagined Steve! Here he is, you know, this kinda country club Chamber of Commerce guy, ten years older than me, but a thinker, you know, someone who's been around, and he's just so good. He's a good man and he's good to me and he's good *for* me.

[BARBARA. That's great, Karen —]

KAREN. He's got this great business and it's because he has these great ideas and he's unafraid to make his ideas realities, you know, he's not afraid of *doing*. I think men on the whole are better at that than women, don't you? *Doing*, just jumping in and *doing*, right or wrong, we'll figure out what it all means later. And the best thing about him, the best thing about him for me, is that now what I think about is *now*. I live *now*. My focus, my life, my world is *now*. I don't give a care about the past anymore, the mistakes I made, the way I *thought*, I won't go back there. And I've realized you can't plan the future, because as soon as you do, you know, something happens, some terrible thing happens —

[BARBARA. *Like your father drowning himself.*

KAREN. *Exactly! Exactly, that's exactly what I mean!*] That's not something you plan for! There's no contingency; you take it as it comes, here and now! Steve had a very important presentation today, for some bigwig government guys who could be very important for his business, something he's been putting together for months, and as soon as we heard about Daddy, he called and canceled his meeting. He has his priorities straight. And you know what the kicker is? *(Barbara waits.)* Do you know what the kicker is?

[BARBARA. *What's the kicker?*]

KAREN. We're going to Belize on our honeymoon.

AUGUST: OSAGE COUNTY

BY TRACY LETTS

VIOLET WESTON — Bev's wife, 65 years old

SYNOPSIS: A vanished father. A pill-popping mother. Three sisters harboring shady little secrets. When the large Weston family unexpectedly reunites after dad disappears, their Oklahoman family homestead explodes in a maelstrom of repressed truths and unsettling secrets. Mix in Violet, the drugged-up, scathingly acidic matriarch, and you've got an unflinching — and uproariously funny — portrait of the dark side of the Midwestern American family.

PLACE: A large country home outside Pawhuska, Oklahoma, sixty miles northwest of Tulsa.

TIME: August 2007.

(Violet sits, exhales. Karen picks up a hand cream from the bedside table, rubs it on her hands.)

VIOLET. You girls all together in this house. Just hearing your voices outside the door gives me a warm feeling. These walls must've heard a lot of secrets.
[KAREN. I get embarrassed just thinking about it.
VIOLET. *Oh ... nothing to be embarrassed about.]* Secret crushes, secret schemes ... province of teenage girls. I can't imagine anything more delicate, or bittersweet. Some part of you girls I just always identified with ... no matter how old you get, a woman's hard-pressed to throw off that part of herself. *[(To Karen, regarding the hand cream.) That smells good.*
KAREN. *Doesn't it? It's apple. You want some?*
VIOLET. *Yes, please. (Karen passes the hand cream to Violet.)]* I ever tell you the story of Raymond Qualls? Not much story to it. Boy, I had a crush on him when I was thirteen or so. Real rough-look-

ing boy, beat-up Levis, messy hair. Terrible underbite. But he had these beautiful cowboy boots, shiny chocolate leather. He was so proud of those boots, you could tell, the way he'd strut around, all arms and elbows, puffed-up and cocksure. I decided I needed to get a girly pair of those same boots and I knew he'd ask me to go steady, convinced myself of it. He'd see me in those boots and say, "Now there's the gal for me." Found the boots in a window downtown and just went crazy: I'd stay up late in bed, praying for those boots, rehearsing the conversation I was going to have with Raymond when he saw me in my boots. Must've asked my momma a hundred times if I could get those boots. "What do you want for Christmas, Vi?" "Momma, I'll give all of it up just for those boots." Bargaining, you know? She started dropping hints about a package under the tree she had wrapped up, about the size of a boot box, real nice wrapping paper. "Now, Vi, don't you cheat and look in there before Christmas morning." Little smile on her face. Christmas morning, I was up like a shot, boy, under the tree, tearing open that box. There was a pair of boots, all right … men's work boots, holes in the toes, chewed-up laces, caked in mud and dog shit. Lord, my momma laughed for days.

BE AGGRESSIVE

BY ANNIE WEISMAN

LAURA — A 17-year-old girl.

SYNOPSIS: Vista Del Sol is a paradise of sandy beaches and avocado-tree-lined streets. But everything changes for seventeen-year-old cheer-leader Laura when her mother is killed in a car crash and she is thrust into the role of caregiver for her younger sister, Hannah, and her brittle father, Phil. Escape comes in the form of Leslie, a ferocious fellow cheer-leader. Leslie has a brochure about the Spirit Institute of the South, a two-week intensive where they can learn real cheer, the kind with Bible-belt intensity. All they need is two weeks and a thousand bucks.

Leslie gets her money easily, manipulating her overwrought single mother, but Laura has it harder and finally steals the money. Armed with only a Mobil card, the girls face the open road together while their frantic parents search for them. When Laura and Leslie finally arrive at their destination, they discover the brochure is twenty years old. In the void of the abandoned schoolyard, Laura finally confronts her mother's loss.

PLACE: Vista Del Sol, a community by the sea in Southern California, and on the road.

TIME: The present.

LAURA.   Is that all there is to say? 'Cuz that doesn't mean any-thing. *(She stares at the brochure.)* In 1971, I wasn't even around yet. But that's when she was really alive, I think. She had a grey streak in the front of her hair. Premature grey. She had it for years until she finally got sick of the giggles and stares and she dyed it like the rest of them. I don't even remember barely. I was so little. She used to tell us things, but I barely remember and I can't ask her again! I can't say, "Hey, Mom, tell me things I never listened to! Tell me how to do things! Tell me how to bake sugar cookies so they're soft in the middle! Tell me how to sweep my hair up so it holds with just a pin. Tell me what it feels like when your water breaks and a baby comes out! I don't have anybody to tell me that! *(Laura starts to tear the brochure.)* I hate my dad! I'm sorry, but I hate him so much! How could he just keep going? I don't understand how he could just keep going! *(Beat.)* Is that what happens? You're young, and you believe in things, and then you, what? You get married, you have kids, you move into a Spanish stucco ocean view unit and you forget? One day you wear your white streak like a peacock's tail, and the next day you're letting them paint it with bleach and toner and wrap it in tin foil and sitting under a hair dryer to cook for an hour while you learn lip-lining tips from a beauty magazine! Like everybody else! When you sit under those dryer domes, you can't see or hear a thing. You just have to sit there quietly and let all that stuff soak into you. *(Beat.)* She's really kind of been gone for a long long time. *(Laura finishes tearing the brochure and starts to scatter the pieces.)* I don't want to be a dead girl. I want to be a person who's alive.

BEAUTIFUL CHILD

BY NICKY SILVER

NAN — Isaac's mother.

SYNOPSIS: Can we love someone whose actions fall outside our moral code? BEAUTIFUL CHILD presents Harry and Nan, a couple whose marriage has become a comfortable battleground of witty barbs and infidelity. Everything they think they know, however, is called into question when their son, Isaac, an art teacher and painter, comes for lunch and asks if he can stay. The world's no longer safe for Isaac, as his secrets are about to become public: he has fallen in love, and has been having an affair, with one of his students, an eight-year-old boy named Brian. Harry and Nan search for clues, desperate to make sense of this horror, alternately looking for exoneration and punishment for what must be their fault. They want to help their son, and they want to love him. But how? And what is their responsibility to the world and to the children in Isaac's future?

PLACE: The living room of an elegant home and a section of patio that may always be present or glide on and off.

TIME: The present.

NAN. I was happy. He wanted me to visit. I went to his home, that apartment, the smells, turpentine and chemicals. I can smell them. It's early in the morning and he's half asleep. We go to breakfast ... I'm so happy. He's just started, at that school, that school in the brownstone. He's so excited. He asks me if I want to watch, if I want to come and watch him teach. I can't imagine it's appropriate, but I do, I want to. I want to see what he's become. He tells me that it's fine, that it's nothing. That they're very informal. So I do, I go, I sit in the back, in a tiny toy desk, feeling foolish and proud as my son does his job, walking among the students, who are so little, seven, eight, nine. He hands out praise and advice — mostly praise, and guides their hands, which hold giant brushes and make circles and straight lines in all different colors. And they laugh and they love him and he's good at his job ... Then, after the class the children wash up. And most of them leave, some faster than others, but one little boy. I hear his name.

[HARRY. (Softly.) Don't.]

NAN. Victor. His name was Victor. And he waited, still sitting, until Isaac came over and looked at his work. Isaac knelt down, next to him, this perfect child, and put his hand, which seemed so huge, on the tiny shoulder. He talked to him, too softly for me to hear, until he smiled, Victor smiled and blushed and looked at his painting, which I couldn't make out from the back of the room. Then Isaac, our son, moved his hand from the shoulder, and placed his hand on the back of his head, the child's head, and then on his cheek, on his mouth, until he lifted his eyes, the child, and looked at our son ... And they didn't speak. They looked at each other, too closely. Like lovers. Heat and fear and so much sadness in the air between them. And I knew. I knew. I knew what it was. There was nothing else that it could be.

BEAUTY ON THE VINE

BY ZAK BERKMAN

LAUREN — Early to mid-20s.

SYNOPSIS: From mixed-race identities to extreme plastic surgery, BEAUTY ON THE VINE is a modern fable exploring the power of the human face in hothouse America. When a young female star of right-wing radio is brutally murdered, her husband and father investigate the reasons behind the violence. They discover a world where young women transform themselves to look like their idols, and mothers lose their daughters to the illusion of popularity and power.

LAUREN. *(On radio.)* I was at the grocery store and a fat woman walked by me. Very fat with a bad dye job, black spandex jogging shorts, too much eye shadow — and she wore a red T-shirt with big lettering that said "All American Mom." No irony. She was mad proud of being who she was: fat, ugly, poorly dressed. There are a lot of these people in our country. Thinking it's okay to be lazy and stupid. *(Daniel listens to the recording on a CD player in the conference room. A box of CDs is in front of him.)* How did we get this way? Have we been so brainwashed by the liberal elite telling us we're all equal — that we all deserve the same amount of space and time in their history books — that we think it's okay now to be fat slobs? It's this kind of thinking that's destroying America — all these do-gooders on the Left, with their arsenal of guilt-trips and obsessions with empathy — they've taken away the meaning of greatness. They've made the mediocre and even the evil … acceptable. But they're wrong. We're *not* all equal. We're not all the same. *(A Woman who looks very much like Lauren walks past the conference room. Sweet notices her. Another Woman walks past in the opposite direction, again she is strikingly similar to Lauren. On radio:)* Those poor and disenfranchised suicide bombers are *still* terrorists. Those child-abused serial killers on death row are *still* murderers. And that fat mom is *still* going to die of heart disease or diabetes when she's fifty, leaving her kids with a legacy of resentment and medical bills. Empathy is useless. Some of us *are* better. Am I right?

23

BHUTAN

BY DAISY FOOTE

MARY — The mother.

SYNOPSIS: BHUTAN follows a New England family's ups and downs after the death of their father. Frances Conroy wonders how she ended up here. Her mother is driving her crazy. Her aunt is stalking a married man. Her brother is in prison. She dreams of Bhutan but can barely find the kitchen door.

PLACE: Tremont, New Hampshire.

TIME: End of September, present year.

MARY. You watch your mouth, mister. *(He starts to cry. She puts her arm around him.)* You're going to get over this girl. You are. You'll graduate this spring, you'll start working for Joe full-time. And eventually you'll either partner with him or start a business of your own. You'll meet a girl, the right girl, you'll have kids. And maybe, just maybe I'll give you five or six acres of my own land. You can build a house on it and then I can really make your life miserable, telling you how to raise your kids, telling your wife what she's doing wrong.
[WARREN. No, Anna's the one.
MARY. She's not ...
WARREN. She is ... I know it ... (Mary makes him look at her.)]
MARY. When this town first started changing and all these new people were moving in, your father, he was glad for all the business, but he'd always say, "I could be the goddamn plumbing king, Mares. Build my million-dollar house on the top of the highest point in town. And these new people, these lawyers and MBAs and doctors, they'll chat with me while I fix their toilets and their pipes, they might offer me a beer and ask me about my wife and kids, but they won't ever, ever invite me to one of their cocktail parties or to go skiing for a weekend or to their daughter's wedding." But then your father wasn't interested in spending time with them either. He was

more than glad to take their money but beyond that, they bored him to tears. *(A beat.)* There are differences, Warren. People might say the world isn't like that now. All part of one big pot. But that isn't true. There are people who take African safaris and people who know that doing something like that is a complete waste of time and money. And you don't do African safaris, son. You never have and you never will. I'm not saying that my marriage with your father was perfect. There were times I would look at him and think, "How the hell did I end up with this jerk?" But I understood him and he understood me. It was deep inside us, a kind of shorthand. You need a girl who understands you that way. A girl who knows that when you get home at night, you might be too tired to go to a party, too tired to play with your kids, too tired to fix the goddamn dryer. That you might just want to sit in front of the TV and not say a word.

A BICYCLE COUNTRY

BY NILO CRUZ

INES — A woman in her 30s.

SYNOPSIS: Ines, Julio and Pepe, whose lives seem to be moving nowhere, set out to build a dream, even if that dream seems perilous. This stirring portrait of three Cuban exiles and their harrowing journey across the Caribbean Sea examines the universal themes of freedom and oppression, hope and survival.

PLACE: A raft on the sea.

TIME: Before the U.S. intervention on Cuban rafters.

INES. Come on and dance with me. *(Ines pulls his arm to dance.)*
[JULIO. Dance with him.]
INES. You have to dance.
[JULIO. I can't dance. I don't know how to dance.]
INES. Oh come on!
[JULIO. No ... no dancing ...
INES. You're lying. You can dance.
JULIO. You're crazy. I don't want to dance.]
INES. Well, I won't force you. I'll leave you alone because it's your birthday. *(Pause.)*

   I went real far to get this rum. I know this is the one you like.
   I wanted this day to be special.
[JULIO. (Pours more rum in her glass.) You want more, Pepe?
PEPE. Sure. (Toasting.) "To your health! We would all like something better. Life is like that. We all want something better."

   See, I'm getting better at this. (They drink.)]
INES. Play music, Pepe. We'll dance. Oh, I can feel the rum rising to my face. *(Pepe switches on the radio. An old bolero plays.)*

   Leave that song on! I love old music. I used to collect music like this one. Oh! I collected all kinds of things ...

   Oh! So many things gone. Got rid of everything ... All of it gone ... *(Dances by herself.)* Gave everything away ...

I thought I was going to leave this place. But it never happened. *(The rum makes her giddy. She laughs.)*

I was stupid. Gone mad in the head. And all for a German tourist. With him I went to all the nightclubs. I wore sunglasses and pretended to be a foreigner. All the waiters thought I was from Brazil, Italy, Portugal, until the German would get stuck ordering something, and I would have to open my mouth. *(She laughs at herself.)*

He was gone at the end of summer … August … September … Gone away … *(She becomes bitter.)* Like all foreigners, they leave when the seaweed comes to the shores. The scum of the sea. He left dressed the same way I met him, starched white shirt … I stayed a mess, a shipwreck … *(Determined.)* — Oh, I'd like to live in a place where the land extends and I can walk for miles, where I can run and never reach the end.

Here, there's always the sea. The jail of water. Stagnant. Just the sea — Oh, this rum is going to my head, Pepe. *(Ines stops dancing and goes to the table.)* Are you happy, Julio? Are you happy on your birthday?

BLACK SHEEP

BY LEE BLESSING

ELLE — 20s, Max's friend.

SYNOPSIS: A prominent family's "black sheep" nephew, Carl, the son of an interracial marriage, comes to stay with them after being released from prison. But does the family want him? And what does he want from them? In this dark comedy, issues of race, sex and family values play out with wildly comic and disturbing results.

TIME: The present.

(A poolside area on the estate. Elle and Carl sit in lounge chairs. She's in a bathing suit. He's in shorts and a shirt. Light reflects off an unseen pool.)

ELLE. I had the strangest dream last night. Do you dream? I only have nightmares. At least, I never remember happy dreams. Last night I dreamt that Max and I were in the guest house on the floor, and we were — *(Recoiling at the recollection.)* Oh, ugh. Oh … oh — ugh. Ugh! Why do we dream, Carl? I mean, why do we? *(After a beat.)* Max isn't so bad. It's just that he wants to make movies. And he's rich, so he can waste his time any way he wants. At first he got his father's friends to invest in movies he directed himself. Small budgets — a few million, nothing more — but still. They stunk so bad. Not horrendous. I mean, everybody's movies stink a little, right? That's just how movies are — they stink a little. But his. Really stunk. I should know, I'm in the business. I was the slutty one in *All The President's Hookers?* Did you see that? Not in prison I guess. Anyhow, by the time I met Max he was in another end of the industry. We hit it off right away. As friends, I mean. If he wants to nail me, we've gotta be married. I'm not like the other girls he's had — I get a ring. I mean, look at all this shit around here. Wouldn't you hold out? Max's family made some of their money in diamonds. Can you imagine the fucking ring? It's gonna happen, too. He really wants to do me. It's almost funny.

THE BOOK OF LIZ

BY AMY SEDARIS and DAVID SEDARIS

SISTER ELIZABETH DONDERSTOCK — 50 to 60 years old.

SYNOPSIS: Sister Elizabeth Donderstock is Squeamish, and has been her whole life. She makes cheese balls that sustain the existence of her entire religious community, Clusterhaven. However, she feels unappreciated among her Squeamish brethren, and she decides to try her luck in the outside world. Along the way, she meets a Cockney-speaking Ukrainian immigrant couple who find her a job waiting tables at Plymouth Crock, a family restaurant run almost entirely by recovering alcoholics. The alcoholics love her. The customers love her. Things are going great for Liz, until she's offered a promotion to manager. Unfortunately, Liz has a sweating problem, and to get the job, she'll have to fix it. Meanwhile, back at Clusterhaven, Liz's compatriots just can't seem to duplicate her cheese ball recipe, and it's going to cost them their quaint, cloistered lifestyle. They are panic-stricken and desperate, and sure she sabotaged the recipe. Does Liz go through with the operation? Can the Squeamish be saved? Will the cheese balls ever taste good again?

ELIZABETH. The stars are out and you can see the constellations quite clearly. There's Orion, Calpurnia, and the tip of Feces. We used to lie out on this very lawn and study them for hours. Remember those days, Joshua? That was back when you called it the sky rather than the heavens. Back when you could look up at one thing without looking down on another. Is it just me, or does that seem like a thousand years ago? I remember one time — oh, we were young then — Sister Lacy, the schoolmarm, told us to pick something we loved, aside from God, and list ten things that were wrong with it. You picked the moon and said it was conceited and judgmental and just plain mean. Remember that? I wanted to prove you wrong and so, one afternoon — oh, it was hot — one of the dormitories had burned down and while everyone was off saving what they could I took some melted cheese and formed it into a ball thinking that *this, this* was what the moon was really like. Round and perfect at the start. You carve off a little piece every day and then, once you're finished, you replace it with a new one. I made those cheese balls to please you, and then to please God. And that pleased *me* until I found that I was the one being whittled down to nothing. Stick a moon in the sky, put a nice smoky cheese ball on the table, and people will notice when it's waning. But that's not always true of a person, is it? I was chopping walnuts one morning about six months ago and I asked myself *when did this happen? When did I begin to feel so empty and unimportant, and how is it that nobody's noticed it before now? Not even me?* Why is it, old friend, that I had to dress like a peanut in order to feel like a human again?

CAROL MULRONEY

BY STEPHEN BELBER

CAROL MULRONEY — 32, honest, smart, white, depressed by the self-indulgence of her depression; optimistic. Works in a store, paints on her downtime.

SYNOPSIS: Carol Mulroney stands on her roof, watching the sparkling lights of the city below. Her rooftop is her hideaway from the chaotic world below. But the roof is being overrun by the inevitable messiness of life and the people in it. Over the fragmented course of a day, Carol will stay on her roof and seek to make connections with those to whom she is closest. In each encounter she will try to make sense of who she is in relation to these insane, loving, unintentionally hurtful people, and in the end she will find connection on her own defiant terms.

PLACE: A city; the rooftop.

TIME: A Friday in autumn.

(Carol stands alone on a rooftop; the speech is casual, cheery even.)

CAROL. There are two things about a roof that knock me out. The first is the view. I stand up there, up here, at night, and I look at the sparkling lights down below and I feel like I can figure it all out. I feel like the shock of the city and the traffic and the people — all that stuff that slams you in the face when you get too close — that it somehow becomes beautiful. Uncompromisingly beautiful. *(Pause.)* Because when I go down there, when I come down from the roof to buy a box of ... eggs — it's like I suddenly have no idea. The whole thing becomes ... untamed. I go to the store and all I see are the light bulbs, stripped of their uncompromisingly beautiful sparkle. And I feel like I can't figure anything out.

   The other thing about a roof that knocks me out is its edge. Because it scares the shit out of me. I don't like to go near a roof's edge because — I guess this is pretty typical — because I feel like I have the potential to jump. *Is* that typical? I don't know. Part of me knows it is, that it's not uncommon for human beings to have the urge to … fall away. *(Pause.)* And the reason it freaks me out so much is because I don't like having that urge. It's not my natural instinct. My natural instinct, I think, is to connect with people. On a very simple level. To feel that what I want and need in life is somehow aligned with what other people want and need, aligned in such a way that we can all, could all … live together happily. *(Pause.)* And believe me, I'm not one of these people who says no to everything, or who would jump. Because I wouldn't. In fact, I've tended to say yes more than is good for me, but … but it never seems to work out, for me, this desire for alignment. And consequently, as much as I love a roof, my roof, whenever I get too near its edge … I get that urge.

CAVEDWELLER

BY KATE MOIRA RYAN

Based on the novel by Dorothy Allison

DEDE WINDSOR — Teenage daughter of Delia. Likes fast boys and fast cars.

SYNOPSIS: Adapted from the novel by Dorothy Allison, CAVE-DWELLER follows Delia Byrd, the forty-year-old lead singer of the group Mud Dog whose rock-star boyfriend has just died in an accident. She decides to leave Los Angeles and return home to rural Georgia with her teenage daughter, Cissy, in tow. Back in Georgia is the ex-husband, now dying of cancer, and the two daughters, Dede and Amanda, that Delia abandoned fourteen years ago. Dede, who seems most like her mother, is the wild and rebellious one, fast on the road to becoming an alcoholic and the town tramp. Amanda, in contrast, has sublimated her anger into becoming a sanctimonious, Bible-thumping fundamentalist. To rebuild a family from the ruins she left behind, Delia has her work cut out for her, but in those ruins and in that work lies the promise of her redemption.

PLACE: Cayro, Georgia.

TIME: 1981–1986.

(Cayro County Jail. Dede sits at a table with Delia.)

DEDE. Fucking waitress that served me beer and chicken wings, and him DOING HER LIKE THAT! Saying he loves me and then two of them together. I knew it was a trick all along. She wasn't just there to pick up keys to Biscuit World. She wasn't just there doing him a favor. Oh, no. I went back to apologize and then I saw her at the door. Looking at him like he was one of *People* magazine's Most Handsome Men Ever. The gun was under the seat of my car, the one I got after Billy Tucker scared me. I don't even remember going for it. Seemed like I was watching them and then I was shooting. "You want to marry me?" I shouted and shot him. If Nolan loved me right, this would have never happened. If Nolan loved me right, he would have left things alone. I told him to let it alone. You think about how I felt, believing him, trusting him, letting myself love him, and him to do me like that? I trusted him. I trusted him. *(Delia sits down.)* So how is he. He dead yet?

DEN OF THIEVES

BY STEPHEN ADLY GUIRGIS

BOOCHIE — Topless dancer, 20s/30s

SYNOPSIS: Maggie is a junk-food–binging shoplifter looking to change her life. Paul is her formerly four-hundred-pound compulsive-overeating sponsor in a twelve-step program for recovering thieves. Flaco, Maggie's jealous ex-boyfriend, is a charismatic wannabe Puerto Rican small-time thief, who spins a grammatically challenged but persuasive yarn about seven hundred and fifty thousand dollars in unprotected drug money sitting in a safe in a downtown disco. This would-be criminal crew is rounded out by Flaco's new girlfriend, Boochie — a mala-prop-slinging topless dancer. When things don't go according to plan, this hapless quartet finds themselves at the mercy of Louie "The Little Tuna" Pescatore, a reluctant heir to the criminal empire run by his father — "The Big Tuna" — who has left him in charge for the week-end. The penalty for stealing from The Tuna is death. But Louie offers them a break: "I need one body and three thumbs, you can choose the who, whys and wherefores among yourselves." Tied to chairs and able to move only their mouths, they must now fight for their lives by out-arguing each other as to who deserves to live.

BOOCHIE. Thank you. *(She clears her throat.)* Society would suffer if I die for many multiples of reasons. Number one: As a exotic dancer, I bring smiles to the faces of many sad lonely mens, and sometimes womens too if they into that. Number three: I am extremely fly — as you definitely noticed — maybe in the top ten of flyest womens in the city, and if they serious about keeping New York beautiful then they gotta need me around, right? … I'm also a sexual surrogate, which means I fuck for educationalism, which is important to society since I teach mens to fuck better, and God knows womankind could use more mens who fuck better — right, Maggie? I provide that. I also teach fellatios to the womens which I'm sure most mens could appreciate … Number eight: I believe in charity. When I get famous, I plan on donating a lot of money to the Ronald McDonald House so sick children of all ages could always eat McDonald's for free, so even when they die, they'll die happy. Oh, also I belong in the A.S.P.C.A. ... *(Pause.)* One more thing, which, I don't even know why I'm saying this, but, I got abused a lot as a child, people. A lot. And I ain't sayin' that for you to feel sorry for me, even though I wouldn't mind if you did feel sorry so I could be one a the survivors, but, the point of this is that everyone in my family called me "garbage can," including my mother, which I think dat ain't very nice, but also I think is very false 'cuz I ain't no fuckin' garbage can! And even though I gots lots and lots of talents which make me definitely a big bargain for the society, even if I didn't have *any* of those amazing skills and dreams which I, like, process — even if I *was* a garbage can — which I'm not — I'd still be valuable 'cuz where you gonna put your garbage if you don't got no can? Someone's gotta be that can, right? So, for all these ideals and many more, I feel I am a valuable ass to society and many, many peoples of all the five boroughs, and maybe even the world, would have their lives be more messed up if I wasn't around to be around ... Dass it. Thank you.

THE DIXIE SWIM CLUB

BY JESSIE JONES, NICHOLAS HOPE, JAMIE WOOTEN

VERNADETTE SIMMS — 50s. A hard-luck case if there ever was one. Marriage and motherhood came shortly after college; a dark cloud has hovered above her ever since. A public school teacher, with limited finances and a problematic home life in Spivey's Corner, North Carolina, Vernadette is self-deprecating by necessity. She faces her tribulations with gallows humor and the unwavering support of lifelong friends.

SYNOPSIS: Five Southern women, whose friendships began years ago on their college swim team, set aside a long weekend every August to recharge those relationships. Free from husbands, kids and jobs, they meet at the same beach cottage on North Carolina's Outer Banks to catch up, laugh and meddle in each other's lives. As the years pass, these women increasingly rely on one another, to get through the challenges life flings at them. And when fate throws a wrench into one of their lives in the second act, these friends rally 'round their own with the strength and love that takes this comedy in a poignant and surprising direction.

PLACE: The living room of a beach cottage on the Outer Banks of North Carolina.

TIME: A weekend in August, 32 years after their college graduation.

VERNADETTE. Alright, that's it. That is it! I'm gonna have to clarify something the tofu has obviously leached from your good sense. Biscuits are the ultimate Southern comfort food, so fat and carbs do not count. They're what I ate when I was sick or lonely and when company came to dinner and after we opened our presents on Christmas morning. My mama made them, and her mama before her and my great grandmama before her and I bet the same can be said for every one of us in this room. *The New York Times* is not going to take away this Southern girl's biscuits!
[SHEREE. Vernadette, just calm down —]

VERNADETTE. Oh, we are way past the time for calm. You and your upscale, *Times*-readin', sprout-eatin' kind need to wake up. People who don't give a damn about our culture or our way of life are paving over our farms and building suburbs and coffee bars and super centers that suck the life out of every main street in every small town. And they won't stop until they've made this country one big, homogenous, soulless blur. Well, I'm not going to be quiet about it anymore. They can take away our cotillions, they can laugh at us for using the word "y'all," they can even build strip malls on our battlefields. But as long as there is music in Memphis, as long as a peanut grows in Georgia, as long as I am alive and can remember the South of my childhood, there will be biscuits on my table! And the day I stop eatin' 'em will be the day they pry 'em out of my cold, dead Southern hands!

EVERYTHING WILL BE DIFFERENT

BY MARK SCHULTZ

CHARLOTTE — 15 or thereabouts.

SYNOPSIS: Teenage Charlotte's beautiful mother is dead, and in the midst of her own grief and her father's unwillingness to cope, she turns for comfort to the story of Helen of Troy, convinced that beauty, desire and fame can help her bring her mother back and punish the world that took her away in the first place. Getting beauty tips from her popular friend, seeking career advice on how to be a porn star from a guidance counselor who may or may not be having an affair with her, and searching for love from the football jock who may barely even know she exists, Charlotte finds herself searching in fantasy for what she cannot find in reality.

TIME: The present.

CHARLOTTE. I am so resolved. I am so ready. There is a world and I will see it. And you won't stop me. I will have adventures. I will be like an explorer. I will make new friends. I will fall in love. I will be like Christopher Columbus or Francis Drake or like Magellan or whatever. Because there is a world and I am determined. And when I come back? If I come back? No one will recognize me. I will be like a movie star or like a famous person and no one will recognize me and I will see through everyone. I will see through everyone. Even you. I will look right through you and you will look at me, and you'll think to yourself who the hell is that and I'll just smile at you. I'll just smile and I'll mumble something like profound or something really famous like a famous something like what someone famous would say because that's who I'll be because I'll know a lot more, I'll know a hell of a lot more when I come back. Or maybe I'll just say, "Fuck you" because I can see through you. Fuck you. Under my breath. To the wall. To the fucking wall. I'll see through you to the fucking wall and you won't even know that you're nothing to me. And I'll say fuck you and you'll think Is she talking to me? and you won't even know. You are a ghost to me. And I don't care. Everyone a fucking ghost. Everyone. And I'm the only one. I'm the only one who means more than you or anyone else.

FABULATION

OR, THE RE-EDUCATION OF UNDINE

BY LYNN NOTTAGE

UNDINE — 37.

SYNOPSIS: FABULATION is a social satire about an ambitious and haughty African-American woman, Undine Barnes Calles, whose husband suddenly disappears after embezzling all of her money. Pregnant and on the brink of social and financial ruin, Undine retreats to her childhood home in Brooklyn's Walt Whitman projects, only to discover that she must cope with a crude new reality. Undine faces the challenge of transforming her setbacks into small victories in a battle to reaffirm her right to be.

PLACE: New York City.

TIME: The present.

UNDINE. I've never heard anyone say, "I'm happy," and actually feel it. People around me say it automatically in response to "How are you doing?" But when you say it, I'm looking at you, I believe you actually mean it. And I find that reassuring. *(The addicts slowly shift their attention to Undine and Guy.)*
[GUY. Why?]
UNDINE. Because mostly I feel rage. *(Undine realizes the addicts are eavesdropping and finds herself including them in her confessional.)* Anger, which I guess is a variation of rage and sometimes it gives way to panic, which in my case is also a variation of rage. I think it's safe to say that I have explored the full range of rage. And it has been with me for so long, that it's comforting. I'm trying to move beyond it, sometimes I even think I have, but mostly I'm not a very good human being. Sometimes I'm less than human, I know this, but I can't control it. I killed my family. *(A collective gasp.)* Yes, I killed them. It was on the day of my college graduation. Dartmouth. My family drove 267 miles in a rented minivan,

41

loaded with friends and relatives eager to witness my ceremony. They were incredibly proud, and why not? I was the first person in the family to graduate from college. They came en masse, dressed in their Alexander's best. Loud, overly eager, lugging picnic baskets filled with fragrant ghetto food ... let's just say their enthusiasm overwhelmed me. But I didn't mind, no, I didn't mind until I over-heard a group of my friends making crass unkind comments about my family. They wondered aloud who belonged to *those* people. It was me. I should have said so. I should have said that my mother took an extra shift so I could have a new coat every year. My father sent me ten dollars every week, his Lotto money. But instead I locked myself in my dorm room and refused to come out to greet them. And I decided on that day, that I was Undine Barnes, who bore no relationship to those people. I told everyone my family died in a fire, and I came to accept it as true. It was true for years. Understand, Sharona had to die in a fire in order for Undine to live. At least that's what I thought. What I did was awful, and I'm so so sorry. And, Guy, you are such a good, decent man. And I wouldn't blame you if you walked away right now. But I don't want you to. I feel completely safe with you.

[GUY. *That is a good thing.*]

UNDINE. I am not yet divorced, I'm being investigated by the FBI, I'm carrying the child of another man and I'm not really a junkie. (*A collective gasp from the addicts.*) Are you still happy?

FLESH AND BLOOD

BY PETER GAITENS

Adapted from the novel by Michael Cunningham

MARY — a mother of adult children.

SYNOPSIS: FLESH AND BLOOD, adapted from Pulitzer Prize–winning novelist Michael Cunningham's saga of twentieth-century American life, traces nearly 100 years in the lives of one archetypal family. Dominated by their volatile father, the Greek immigrant Constantine, and alienated from their mother, the genteel and ambitious Mary, the Stassos children, Susan, Billy and Zoe, struggle to build lives and find love in a culture undergoing tectonic shifts. Like lonely planets whose long, elliptical orbits collide in unexpected, sometimes violent ways, the members of the Stassos family, careen both towards and away from one another in poignant, heartbreaking and sometimes shattering fashion.

PLACE: A garden.

MARY. *(Touches the pearls at her throat. She turns to the audience.)* We have all lived to this point. Just now we find ourselves here, under a huge gray sky, at the tip of this island, with the harbor before us and the names of the dead at our backs. And what happens now? I have a ticket for Paris and a plastic bag full of ashes in my purse. Just some ashes. They're going a number of different places. As you can imagine, the instructions were quite specific. Other friends and relations have other destinations; I was told to take these to Paris. It seems I'm going to be scattering them in the Seine, in the Luxembourg Gardens, and in a certain bar where I will be very, very out of place. I am, of course, going to do it. I'm not the least bit afraid. When I come back home, I'm going to put the house on the market. I'm going to stop coloring my hair. But right now? Right *now?* Here we are. We four. A divorced woman and her son and his husband and the grieving, furious little boy we all intend, somehow, to try and raise. I can love this. I can try. I can try and love this. There's nothing else for me to do. For this *is* what the living do. Here are the years to come. One hour and then another and another and another and another.

[*HARRY. Let's go.*]

MARY. This isn't the end. It never is. It's the middle. It's the beginning. It all depends on when you came in and when you have to go.

FROZEN

BY BRYONY LAVERY

AGNETHA — 30s/40s.

SYNOPSIS: One evening ten-year-old Rhona goes missing. Her mother, Nancy, retreats into a state of frozen hope. Agnetha, an American academic, comes to England to research a thesis: "Serial Killing — A Forgivable Act?" Then there's Ralph, a loner who's looking for some distraction. Drawn together by horrific circumstances, these three embark on a long, dark journey which finally curves upward into the light. Angry, humane and compassionate, FROZEN is an extraordinary play that entwines the lives of a murderer, the mother of one of his victims and his psychologist to explore our capacity for forgiveness, remorse and change after an act that would seem to rule them out entirely.

PLACE: On an airplane to England.

TIME: The present.

AGNETHA.
(Keys.)
    "Serial Killing ... a forgivable act?"
(She drains her drink. Presses the "Flight Attendant" summoning light ... no response ... Keys.)
    "Judicial Revenge ... a political choice?"
(Pours non-existent drops of liquid from two or three small in-flight bottles of brandy into the glass. Presses Flight Attendant Call again ... no response. Keys.)
    Brandy Refill ... a Forlorn Hope?
    Yes ... I think so ... Close File ... Save? ...
    shit ... E Mail ... oh yes please ...
(She starts writing furiously ...)
    Dear David,
    Dearest Damn Fuck You Then David
    I hate you
    I hate hate hate hate hate you

45

All the people on this flight are in mortal danger and
it is your fault.
You will be responsible for these multiple deaths
as we plummet out of the sky
into the sea a very very very long way down there
right under where I am sitting.
on *big* air
over *big* sea
it is your fault
you and your Big News
you and your Hilarious Damn Bad Behaviour have
alchemised me into
Miss Fudge Feeling of Washington Square
who is shit-scared of flying!
Give me back my real brain!
Hand over my native intelligence!
when we crash
because of you
because of you taking away my faith in anything at all …
I take innocent people with me …
Lily-White Souls perish here …
(She pours a non-existent drop of brandy into her glass.)
although the stewardess serving me deserves to die …
a lonely, painful, lingering, agonising death
for the impressive number of
times she has willfully ignored my request for brandy
and for a certain radiant spitefulness over her
inability to provide me with a vegetarian meal …
I imagine pouncing,
sinking my teeth into her neck just above her
white pretty blouse and biting out her throat
murmuring all the time
"How's *this* for going with
The Meat Option?"
*(She covers her laptop screen with a "don't copy my homework" arm,
against her next-door neighbour. Looks out of the window.)*
Still over sea.

Watery death for us all then …
Lovely, violent in-flight movie

Many good and worthless men perished
in explosions of bright red blood.

I thought of you.

THE GOAT OR,
WHO IS SYLVIA?

BY EDWARD ALBEE

STEVIE — Martin's wife.

SYNOPSIS: THE GOAT OR, WHO IS SYLVIA? is the tale of Martin, a married, middle-aged architect whose life crumbles when he falls in love with a goat named Sylvia. Through showing this family in crisis, Albee challenges audience members to question their own morality in the face of other social taboos including infidelity, homosexuality, incest and, of course, bestiality.

PLACE: A living room.

TIME: The present.

STEVIE. Well, I laughed, of course: a grim joke but an awfully funny one. "That Ross, I tell you, that Ross! You go too far, Ross. It's funny … in its … awful way, but it's way overboard, Ross!" So, I shook my head and laughed — at the awfulness of it, the absurdity, the awfulness; some things are so awful you have to laugh — and then I listened to myself laughing, and I began to wonder why I *was* — *laughing*. "It's not funny when you come right down to it, Ross." Why *was* I laughing? And just like that *(Snaps her fingers.)* I stopped; I stopped laughing. I realized — probably in the way if you suddenly fell off a building — oh, shit! I've fallen off a building and I'm going to die; I'm going to go splat on the sidewalk; like *that* — that it wasn't a joke at all; it was awful and absurd, but it wasn't a joke. And everything tied in — Ross coming here to interview you yesterday, the funny smell, the Noel Coward bit we did about you having an affair, and with a goat. You said it right out and I laughed. You *told* me! You came right out and fucking *told* me, and I laughed, and I made jokes about going to the feed store and I *laughed*. I fucking laughed! Until it stopped; until the laughter stopped. Until it all came together — Ross' letter and all the rest: that odd smell … the

48

mistress' perfume on you. And so I knew.

[*MARTIN. Stevie, I'm so …]*

STEVIE.   Shut up. And so I knew. And next, of course, came believing it. Knowing it — knowing it's true is one thing, but *believing* what you *know* … well, there's the tough part. We all prepare for jolts along the way, disturbances of the peace, the lies, the evasions, the infidelities — *if* they happen. *(Very offhand.)* I've never had an affair, by the way, all our years together; not even with a cat, or … *any*thing.

GOOD THING

BY JESSICA GOLDBERG

NANCY — Mid-40s, inner-city high-school guidance counselor.

SYNOPSIS: John and Nancy Roy, are forty-something high-school guidance counselors whose marriage is on the rocks, in no small part due to John's infidelity with a student. Dean and Mary are recent graduates struggling to make their way in life. Mary is pregnant, and while Dean works, his younger brother, Bobby, must guard Mary to ensure that she doesn't gain access to his stash of drugs. The catalyst linking these characters is Liz, an Ithaca College dropout who has returned home. Liz has been in love with Dean since high school and finds herself once again seeking the guidance of John Roy as she decides the best course for her life would be to rekindle her relationship with Dean and for the two of them to begin a new life.

PLACE: Somewhere in upstate New York.

TIME: The present.

NANCY. It was just hard today, to see you and the girl, a student, to watch you sing to her, and imagine ...
[JOHN. It wasn't her.]
NANCY. I know it wasn't her, it doesn't matter, to me they are all her, they are all her. *(John nods.)* And what's worse, I feel it all the time now with my own students. They come into the office with their searching, their questions, and I just can't look at them the same way. They were my life, John. I want to give them what I would've given my own, and now, now I look at them and see little slutty home-wreckers. I see everything weak about you, about me, about us. *(John moves his hands over his face.)* I can't help it, I can't stop thinking about it, I can't stop thinking that if we had been able to have a child, she might be that age, and you wouldn't be able to see a girl that way, not if you had your own. But I have to stop thinking like that, I have to stop saying things like "if we had," we couldn't ... I have to get past, I need to, tell me how, please? Tell me, I beg you. Tell me how to get past it, John?

GULF VIEW DRIVE

BY ARLENE HUTTON

MAY — A schoolteacher from Kentucky, in her mid-30s.

SYNOPSIS: The third play in the Nibroc Trilogy, which began with LAST TRAIN TO NIBROC and continued with SEE ROCK CITY. In the first two plays, a young pair of Kentuckians named May and Raleigh meet, fall in love, marry and try to reconcile marital expectations and their opinionated mothers-in-law. In GULF VIEW DRIVE, the time frame has moved to the early 1950s, and May and Raleigh have moved to Florida, where the crush of dreams, families and the turbulence of events just outside their door threaten their comfortable life. Their dream house shrinks as relatives descend, further testing the couple's love as they make unconventional decisions in a changing world.

PLACE: A small island community on the Gulf coast of Florida: the screened-in back porch of a modest cinderblock home.

TIME: 1953–1954.

MAY. Well. *(Treva exits. There is silence for a moment.)* I don't have a job.
[*RALEIGH. You're pulling my leg.*]
MAY. I quit my job.
[*RALEIGH. What a day.*]
MAY. I quit my job. I quit my job at school.
[*RALEIGH. Whatever for?*]
MAY. One of my students. Told his parents there was a Negro in his class. And this kid's parents went to the superintendent. Over the principal's head. And the school reprimanded me. For letting a Negro in my classroom.
[*RALEIGH. They can't fire you for that.*]
MAY. Well, they aren't putting me on continuing contract like they were gonna. The assistant principal said I was the best teacher he had, but they couldn't help it.
[*RALEIGH. We'll go to the newspapers. Mack'll help us.*]

MAY. It's all about legality, they said. They said it's not legal.

[RALEIGH. To have a Negro in the classroom?]

MAY. No, they didn't say that. The superintendent's clever. Went all the way to the superintendent, can you imagine? He's clever. Said it wasn't legal for me to have an unregistered student in my class. That I just couldn't admit a student to class on my own, a student who wasn't registered. They said he was too young to be in my class anyway and he wasn't registered. The superintendent says it doesn't make any difference whether he's a Negro or not, of course it does, but they're pretending it doesn't. Said it's all about registering in the proper district.

[RALEIGH. That's nonsense.]

MAY. I said having him in my class was my idea and that his daddy George was against it, but I insisted because I thought the boy was a genius and I wanted him in my classroom.

[RALEIGH. Why would you say that?]

MAY. They were gonna fire George! I couldn't let that happen. I couldn't let them fire George just because I let Lincoln sit in and hear about Shakespeare. So I told them it was all my fault. That I told Lincoln what time to come take out the garbage and that I asked him to stay in my class. And so they aren't going to fire George, just give him a reprimand. I said it was all my idea and if they wanted to keep me from continuing contract over it then I didn't want to teach there anyway. We don't need the money that much, do we?

[RALEIGH. We can get by.]

MAY. I could go teach at a private school, maybe.

[RALEIGH. You don't have to.]

MAY. You should've seen their faces. You know what I said to them? I stood up and I said you are not true educators if you are keeping a child from learning. And then I quit.

HOLD PLEASE

BY ANNIE WEISMAN

ERIKA — 20s.

*SYNOPSIS: Two generations of women, career secretaries in their for-
ties and entry-level assistants in their twenties, gather for a Heart Talk
— an emotional tribunal to record and report sexual harassment.
Leading the charge is Agatha, a bitter secretary determined to bring
the badly behaving bosses to justice. However, Erika, one of the young
assistants, is carrying on an affair with Solomon, the oldest and most
revered of the bosses. Erika is abruptly dumped by Solomon, just as she
discovers that she is pregnant. Soon one of the partners is dismissed for
sexual harassment, and when the new boss arrives, everyone is sur-
prised to learn she is a young woman, who immediately institutes an
efficiency contest. Whoever can demonstrate the most alacrity at their
job wins. But what will happen to the rest of them? Erika has to
decide to stay or go; there is a suggestion that Solomon may have had
affairs before; and when Agatha gets the change she was after, will it
turn out to be better or worse?*

PLACE: An office.

TIME: The present.

ERIKA. His wife is nuts, OK? You should SEE the meds he has
to get for her, the cocktails of anti-psychotics. She drives him
insane! And this is a man who is already under a lot of pressure!
And often in a great deal of pain! I massage his lower back and
that is where he stores a lot of painful memories. He sometimes
shares them with me. *(Beat. Jessica makes a disapproving sound.)*
He's shared A LOT with me. You don't know. And sexually, he's
a completely different person from the one you see in the well-
cut suit, bossing people around. He's the opposite. He's actually
really shy. It's so cute. The first time, he cried a little. I saw tears
in his eyes. I'm telling you, the way he touches me — it's soft, and
gentle. Even when we're only on the Plexiglas floor mat. He's like

a great big little boy. *(Beat.)* His car is huge and powerful, but it has this really quiet engine. Sometimes, afterwards, when he's driving me home, this phrase comes into my head over and over again — "luxury sedan." *(Beat.)* You wouldn't know what I'm talking about.

INTIMATE APPAREL

BY LYNN NOTTAGE

MRS. DICKSON — 50s, African-American. Owner of a boarding-house.

SYNOPSIS: It is 1905 in New York City, where Esther, a black seam-stress, lives in a boarding house for women and sews intimate apparel for clients who range from wealthy white patrons to prostitutes. Her skills and discretion are much in demand, and she has managed to stuff a goodly sum of money into her quilt over the years. One by one, the other denizens of the boarding house marry and move away, but Esther remains, lonely and longing for a husband and a future. Her plan is to find the right man and use the money she's saved to open a beauty parlor where black women will be treated as royally as the white women she sews for. By way of a mutual acquaintance, she begins to receive beautiful letters from a lone-some Caribbean man named George who is working on the Panama Canal. Being illiterate, Esther has one of her patrons respond to the letters, and over time the correspondence becomes increasingly intimate until George persuades her that they should marry, sight unseen.

PLACE: Lower Manhattan.

TIME: 1905.

MRS. DICKSON. I married him, because I was thirty-seven years old, I had no profession and there wasn't a decent colored fella in New York City that would have me.
[ESTHER. But you come to love each other.]
MRS. DICKSON. I suppose. He give me some laughs. But you see, my mother wanted me to marry up. She was a washerwoman, and my father was the very married minister of our mission. He couldn't even look out at her there in the church pews, but she'd sit there proudly every Sunday, determined to gain God's favor. Marry good. She didn't ever want me to be embarrassed of my fingers the way she was of hers. I'd watch her put witch hazel and hot oil on her delicate hands, but they remained raw and chapped and she

kept them hidden inside gray wool gloves. In the winter they'd bleed so bad sometimes, but she'd plunge her hands into the hot water without flinching, knead and scrub the clothing clean. Fold and press for hours and hours, the linen, the bedding, the stockings and the britches, sometimes wearing the frayed gloves so as not to leave bloodstains on her precious laundry. She wouldn't even let me help her, she didn't want my hands to show the markings of labor. I was going to marry up. Love was an entirely impractical thing for a woman in her position. "Look what love done to me," Mama used to say. "Look what love done to me." *(A moment.)* So I did what was necessary to gain favor. I allowed myself to be flattered by gentlemen. You understand? Yes, this "pretty" gal done things, un-pretty things, for this marble mantle, gaslights in every room, a player piano and an indoor toilet.

LAST OF THE BOYS

BY STEVEN DIETZ

LORRAINE — Salyer's mother, 50s.

SYNOPSIS: Ben and Jeeter fought in Vietnam, and for thirty years they have remained united by a war that divided the nation. Joined by Jeeter's new girlfriend and her off-the-grid, whiskey-drinking mother, these friends gather at Ben's remote trailer for one final hurrah. As the night deepens, the past makes a return appearance, and its many ghosts come flickering to life. This is a fierce, funny, haunted play about a friendship that ends — and a war that does not.

PLACE: An abandoned trailer park, somewhere in the Great Central Valley of California.

TIME: The final summer of the twentieth century.

LORRAINE. Yeah, it's weird. Friends are like furniture. When they get old and worn out, you turn the bad side to the wall; cover the stains with pillows. But damned if you don't *sit on 'em anyway. (Beat.)* With women it gets all hinky and complicated — women "move on" or "grow apart" or "have a falling out." But men — I don't know — men just *change bars. (Lorraine lifts her whiskey, drinks. Pause. Then, it just comes out …)* I never told her. I never told Sal about her dad. Whenever she asked, I just said he left me for someone else, because, hey — and I don't care how this sounds — that's exactly what it *felt like. (Beat.)* God, we were *kids.* My Daniel … my Danny was a little boy who got his draft notice. And I was a little girl who couldn't tell him — I put him on that plane and I *never* told him —
[BEN. What?]
LORRAINE. That I had his baby in my gut and not a clue in the world. *(Pause, drinks.)* Left on a Monday. I got some letters from basic training, saying he was shipping out. Next thing I know the Army is calling — telling me my husband is MIA. *Don't I know it,* I said. My Danny's been MIA since he first got his draft notice. We're eighteen years old and he reads that thing and I watch this

... *fog* ... just ... *cover his face.* And I tell him I love him and that I want to spend my life with him, and that ... *fog* ... just ... *does not lift.* To this very day, I listen to people debate that war and what it *did* and what it *meant* and I just want to SHAKE these idiots and make them understand that that war was NOTHING BUT A VAST GLOBAL CONSPIRACY TO *BREAK MY FUCKING HEART. (Pause, still hard.)* As you can see, I'm *over it.* All in the past. Doesn't bother me at all.

LOVE-LIES-BLEEDING

BY DON DeLILLO

LIA — Early 30s, second wife of Alex, an artist.

SYNOPSIS: LOVE-LIES-BLEEDING focuses on the last years of a free-spirited artist, now left invalid after a second stroke. His estranged son, wife and ex-wife struggle over the ultimate question: How do they let him die with dignity? As DeLillo masterfully tackles the ethics of their decision, he amplifies what it truly means to be alive.

SETTING: A spacious room in an old house, remotely located.

(Lia enters and takes up a position behind the lectern.)

LIA. I don't know if it's customary for the wife to speak at a memorial service. The widow. But I came here to say that everything you may believe you know about Alex is only what you know, and it's not everything.

He was not the older man. I was not the younger woman. Can you understand that? The woman half his age, or whatever I was, or whatever he was. We never thought of each other as husband and wife. We were married but we never used those words or fit ourselves into them. I don't know what we were. We were one life, one pulse.

I understand now how two people can live together and when one of them dies, the other has to stop living. The other can't live a single day or a single week. A day may be passable, livable. A week, too long and dark. One dies, the other has to die.

I know people tell stories at these gatherings. I don't want to do that. People tell stories, exchange stories. I don't know any stories. You know things about him that I never knew. This means nothing to me. There are no stories. You're here for the wrong reason. If you're here to honor his memory, it's not his memory, it's your memory, and it's false. There are no stories. There are other things, hard to express, so deep and true that I can't share them, and don't want to. In the end it's not what kind of man he was but simply that he's gone. The stark fact. The thing that turns us into children, alone under the sky.

When it stops being unbearable, it becomes something worse. It becomes the air we breathe. My failure came at the end. He could have gone on, I could not. My weaknesss, my failure, this is what I carry. His life is what I carry, step by step. He left in the arms of Morpheus, god of dreams. I've come all this way to say these things.

You'll leave and forget what I've said and so will I. I'll go back home and climb into the burning hills, where he worked, and scatter his ashes there. He goes nowhere now, into nothing. What powerful work he had it in mind to make. Untitled, unfinished. But not nothing.

LOVE SONG

BY JOHN KOLVENBACH

JOAN — Middle-aged.

SYNOPSIS: Beane is an exile from life — an oddball. His well-mean-
ing sister, Joan, and brother-in-law, Harry, try and make time for him
in their busy lives, but no one can get through. Following a burglary on
Beane's apartment, Joan is baffled to find her brother blissfully happy
and tries to unravel the story behind his mysterious new love, Molly.

PLACE: Beane's apartment.

TIME: The present.

(Beane sits at the table. Joan knocks as she enters through the unlocked
door. She stands just inside. Pause. Beane does not look at her, but he
knows she's there.)

JOAN. *(Sitting at the table with Beane.)* Remember Tim Adair?
(Pause.) [Beane?
BEANE. I remember he broke your heart that time and you wouldn't
come out of your room. That was when Mom couldn't hear you unless
you held her by the ears and screamed into her face.]
JOAN. I wrote his book reports.
[BEANE. (Lifting his head from the table.) Why?]
JOAN. Because I loved him more than life itself.
[BEANE. I guess that's a good reason.]
JOAN. Then he left me for that new girl with the jeans.
[BEANE. What's-her-face.]
JOAN. That night, I was up in my room. [You remember this?] It
was dinner time and Mom kept calling —
[BEANE. "Dinner, hoo-hoo."]
JOAN. (Yeah, god, "hoo-hoo") and I was sitting on the edge of the
bed, and I was Crying. *(Beat.)* Just heaving, you know, the end of the
world, Snot. (You know that thing,) You're crying so hard you can't
make space between the sobs to Breathe. *(Beat.)* I was touching

61

myself. For comfort, I dunno, I had my hands down my pants. *(Beat.)* He had that yellow bicycle.

[*BEANE. Yeah.*]

JOAN. And so there I am keening, and masturbating, I'm sloshing around in six kinds of fluid ... and I can remember Seeing myself. Observing myself from above, looking down at this *puddle*. *(Beat.)* I remember thinking, very distinctly I remember thinking: Look at that. Look at her. How I've been Rendered by this boy. This shallow boy, this Paper Bag has Obliterated me, *look* at that. *(Beat.)* And I said, "This is the last time," out loud, I actually swore to myself, The Last Time that I will be made a *Fool* of by Feelings. *(Beat.)* I zipped up my pants and wiped my face on the sheets and I started my life. *(Pause.)* I jumped my husband yesterday. *(Pause.)* I kissed his feet and made him scream like a baboon and I cried on his shoulder and lay there next to him and traced pictures on his stomach with my finger.

MARIE ANTOINETTE: THE COLOR OF FLESH

BY JOEL GROSS

ELISA — A strikingly beautiful young woman.

SYNOPSIS: MARIE ANTOINETTE: THE COLOR OF FLESH is a dramatic love triangle set during the turbulent years around the French Revolution. Elisabeth Vigée le Brun, a beautiful, social climbing portrait painter, uses her affair with Count Alexis de Ligne, a left-leaning philanderer, to get a commission to paint the naive young Queen Marie Antoinette. While Elisa uses the queen to further her career and Alexis uses the queen to further his political goals, both learn to love the woman they're exploiting. Elisa becomes the queen's best friend, and Alexis becomes the queen's lover. Elisa tries to end the scandalous affair between the queen and Alexis, both out of concern for the queen's political position and jealousy over Alexis' love, until the Revolution shatters all three of their lives.

PLACE: Paris, Versailles and Vienna.

TIME: 1774–1793.

ELISA. Not because of politics! Because of — *(Pause.)* Because of her. *(Explaining.)* I am a painter. A painter is drawn to her subjects by a powerful force. I loved portraits. I loved costumes, brightly colored, of sensuous fabrics. I loved white necks, brilliant jewels, red lips, glittering eyes. I found those subjects in palaces, not in slums. Perhaps that is a crime to you. Certainly it is a crime to those now in power, and who would kill me if they had the chance. But I try not to think about them. Life is too short for what I hope to achieve. *(Pause.)* In the midst of all this madness, I've been studying Rubens' paintings. Learning how to layer a canvas, to leave a glow that shines through walls of paint. To make mortal skin otherworldly, luminous … For what purpose? For beauty. Not to beautify imperfect flesh and bone. But to reveal the beauty that is eternal and perfect. The light that is within. *(Pause.)* Toinette used to say that I was very good with the surface of things. I wish I could paint her now. I would no longer prettify the surface. No matter what the world has done to her, I would make the glow shine through her skin, reveal the goodness of her soul. The world would know who she was, what it meant to be a queen.

MISS WITHERSPOON

BY CHRISTOPHER DURANG

VERONICA — Smart but worried woman, mid-40s to late 50s. Her nickname, we learn, is Miss Witherspoon.

SYNOPSIS: Veronica, already scarred by too many failed relationships, finds the world a frightening place. Skylab, an American space station that came crashing down to Earth, in particular, haunts and enrages her. So she has committed suicide, and is now in what she expected to be heaven but is instead something called the Bardo (the netherworld in Tibetan Buddhism), and the forces there keep trying to make her reincarnate. So far she's thwarted these return visits to earth with a sort of "spiritual otherworldly emergency brake system" she seems to have. She doesn't like being alive, and post-9/11 finds the world even scarier than when she was there. A lovely if strong-willed Indian spirit guide named Maryamma, however, is intent on getting Veronica back to earth so she can learn the lessons her soul is supposed to learn. Veronica — nicknamed "Miss Witherspoon" by Maryamma — didn't expect there to be any afterlife, but if there has to be one, she demands St. Peter and the pearly gates. But Veronica is stuck with Maryamma and reincarnation. Several times in the play Miss W's brake system fails, and she's forced to return to Earth, but each time she keeps killing herself. By the end of the play, however, Maryamma, convinces Miss W that the world is in such a mess that souls "must move through their spiritual evolution faster than they've been doing … they cannot live through eighty and ninety years and only learn tiny, tiny lessons. We need things to move faster!" In the end, Miss W finally agrees to return to earth to help … well, save the planet basically.

PLACE: Earth, and not Earth.

TIME: Recent past, foreseeable future (1998, 2005 and beyond).

(Veronica is found standing in a pool of light. She speaks to the audience.)

VERONICA.   Well, I'm dead. I committed suicide in the 1990s because of Skylab. Well, not entirely, but it's as sensible an explanation as anything.

Most of you don't remember what Skylab was ... I seem to have had a disproportionate reaction to it, most people seemed to have sluffed it off.

Skylab was this American space station, it was thousands of tons of heavy metal, and it got put up into orbit over the Earth sometime in the 70s.

Eventually the people onboard abandoned it, and it was just floating up there; and you'd think the people who put it up there would have had a plan for how to get it back to Earth again, but they didn't. Or the plan failed, or something; and in 1979 they announced that Skylab would eventually be falling from the sky in a little bit — this massive thing the size of a city block might come crashing down on your head as you stood in line at Bloomingdale's or sat by your suburban pool, or as you were crossing the George Washington Bridge, etc. etc.

Of course, STATISTICALLY the likelihood of Skylab hitting you on the head — or rather hitting a whole bunch of you on the head — statistically the odds were small.

But I can't live my life by statistics.

And the experts didn't think it through, I guess. Sure, let's put massive tonnage up in the sky, I'm sure it won't fall down. Sure, let's build nuclear power plants, I'm sure we'll figure out what to do with radioactive waste *eventually.*

Well, you can start to see I have the kind of personality that might kill myself.

I mean, throw in unhappy relationships and a kind of dark, depressive tinge to my psychology, and something like Skylab just sends me over the edge.

"I CAN'T LIVE IN A WORLD WHERE THERE IS SKYLAB!" — I sort of screamed this out in the airport as I was in some endless line waiting to go away to somewhere or other.

So I died sometime in the 90s. Obviously it was a *delayed* reaction to Skylab.

So I killed myself. Anger turned inward, they say. But at least I got to miss 9/11.

If I couldn't stand Skylab, I definitely couldn't stand the sight of people jumping out of windows. And then letters with anthrax postmarked from Trenton. And in some quarters people danced in the streets in celebration. "Oh, lots of people killed, yippee, yippee, yippee." God, I hate human beings. I'm glad I killed myself.

You know, in the afterlife I'm considered to have a bad attitude.

MONTHS ON END

BY CRAIG POSPISIL

HEIDI — 22, Phoebe's younger sister.

SYNOPSIS: In a series of comic scenes we follow the intertwined worlds of a circle of friends and family whose lives are poised between happiness and heartbreak. The circle centers on Phoebe and Ben, who are engaged to be married but have some lingering doubts. Even so, Elaine is jealous of her friends' relationship, especially since none of hers last more than five dates. She's ready to give up on love until she meets Walter, whose only flaw may be that he's married. Heidi, Phoebe's sister, delivers a comic gem of a commencement address in May that starts as a tribute to the graduates' parents but degenerates into a hysterical tirade against them. Phoebe's wedding day meltdown isn't helped by her father, who, trying to calm her fears, tells her to "Pretend you're in an airplane that's crashing ... " Then in August, Heidi and her sister clash as Phoebe learns that her younger sister may outshine her again.

PLACE: A podium at a college graduation.

TIME: May, the present.

("Pomp and Circumstance" plays as the lights come up, and Heidi, a nervous young woman wearing a black graduation robe, enters and crosses to a podium. She carries a small stack of three-by-five note cards, which she refers to as she speaks.)

HEIDI. Welcome. Welcome friends and family, welcome to our teachers ... and welcome to our parents. *(Slight pause.)* The day has finally come. The day this graduating class has been working towards for so many years of hard study. And I think I speak for my entire generation when I say ... thank you. *(Slight pause.)* Thank you to our parents. The people who lit the way. Who loved us and nurtured us. And who now cheer us on as we set out to face the challenges of tomorrow. *(Pause.)*

This class stands before you today poised to — *(The cards in her hand suddenly fly into the air, scattering around the podium. Heidi freezes and then looks at the cards lying around her on the floor. She tries to continue from memory.)* ... ah, poised to take on those challenges. We greet them with open arms. *(Pause.)* We, ah ... stand ... no, um ... *(She glances down to the cards on the ground, turning her head around to try and read some of them.)* It's wonderful for me to be able to stand here like this ... and look out ... Hold on, I'm sorry. *(Heidi stoops down and collects the cards, pulling them together randomly. She stands and smiles nervously at the audience.)*

And in those faces I see hope, idealism and ... no, that's wrong. *(She flips to the next card.)* We have spent four years at this school, studying hard and playing hard. And all of it has been part of our education, because — *(She goes to the next card.)* If you scratch our collective surface ... damn it. I'm sorry. I guess I should have numbered them. *(Next card.)* Welcome. ... no, did that one. *(Next card.)* Because college isn't just about reading Shakespeare or understanding the Theory of Relativity. These four years have been part of our evolution from adolescence to — *(Next card.)* ... a feeling of great loneliness ... *(Pause.)*

I'm very sorry. Just give me another moment. *(Heidi quickly spreads the cards out on the podium and reorders them. She begins again.)* All right ... The day has finally come. The day this class has been working towards for so many years of hard study. And I think I speak for my entire generation when I say ... oh, what's the point? *(Pause.)*

I mean, it's ruined, right? *(Slight pause.)* This is all my parents' fault. I was fine until they came by my room this morning, and my dad says to me, "Make it good, Heidi. Make sure they remember you." *(Slight pause.)* How's this? *(Slight pause.)*

Not that the speech was much good to begin with. I know these things are supposed to have a theme, but ... I mean, it's all been said already, hasn't it? And I'm sorry, but today just doesn't feel that momentous or anything. I know it's the end of one thing and the start of something else, but so what? Everything's like that. *(Slight pause.)* I don't know why I'm up here. I didn't want to give this address. Hell, I didn't even want to come to this college! I liked Vassar! But my dad went here. "It's a great school, Heidi. When you graduate from a place like this you can get a job anywhere." *(Pause.)*

Which would be great, if I had the slightest idea what I wanted to do with my life. *(Slight pause.)* I think that's the symptom of my generation's disease. We're caught between optimism and nihilism.

You raised us to believe in limitless possibility. Consequently we have no idea how to choose anything. *(Slight pause.)* Not that there seems to be much point. The country is, what ... trillions of dollars in debt? And who knows if there will be any social security left by the time I retire, so why think about the future? *(Pause.)*

There'll be peace, you said. And racial harmony, sexual equality. Diseases will vanish. *(Pause.)* Uh-huh. *(Slight pause.)* Yeah, this from the people who were gonna save the world, but then decided to make a bundle on Wall Street instead. Kind of an oxymoron, don't you think, Mom? *(Slight pause.)* Was it too hard? Or did you just get bored? *(Pause.)*

And you wonder why we get tattoos and pierce our belly buttons, or eyebrows, or whatever. We're pissed off because you lied to us. *(Slight pause.)* Well, mainly, we're angry, because you took all the good drugs, had all the good sex, and then made all the good money. *(Slight pause.)* The only thing you're leaving for us is the bill. *(Pause.)*

I should probably stop here. *(Heidi looks over the cards on the podium and chooses one.)* And so, in closing, this class would like to say a heartfelt ... thank you ... to our parents. Thank you for loving us and taking care of us. *(Pause.)* We look forward to returning the favor in thirty or forty years. *(She exits. Fade to black.)*

THE MOONLIGHT ROOM

BY TRISTINE SKYLER

SAL — A girl, 16 years old. Shy, vulnerable.

SYNOPSIS: A dark tale of urban adolescence and family life, THE MOONLIGHT ROOM is set in the emergency room of a New York City hospital as two high school students wait for news on the fate of a friend. As the situation worsens and family members begin to arrive, the play examines the idea of "at-risk" youth, and the potential for risk within your own family.

PLACE: The action takes place in the waiting area of the emergency room of a hospital on the Upper East Side of Manhattan, in New York City.

TIME: The present.

SAL. *(Not angry at Joshua, but sad, confiding her frustration to him.)* What do you know? Your mom's with someone. She's happy. My mom barely goes out. She says she'd rather stay home and clean the apartment. I'm not even allowed to have friends over because they'll interfere with her depression. And she doesn't want to wash her hair. Sometimes she goes a whole week. I tell her that if maybe we had people around she would start to feel better. But she doesn't listen. She'll sit there watching *Jeopardy* and bad-mouth my dad. The same speech I've been hearing since he left. On and on and on and on. And then when he comes over to pick me up, she puts on lipstick! She doesn't wash her hair, and she has on the same outfit she's worn for three days, but she puts on lipstick! I swear one night I'm going to go out, and I'm just not going to come home. *(They sit in silence for a few beats. Sal becomes embarrassed.)* I just don't want to have to call her. *(Pause.)* You don't realize how lucky you are. You do whatever you want. You could come home tomorrow and it's fine. I come home tomorrow and I'm on the back of a milk carton.

A MOTHER'S LOVE

from LIFE IS SHORT

BY CRAIG POSPISIL

MELISSA — 30s/40s.

SYNOPSIS: In a darkly comic monologue, Melissa calmly explains her reasons for taking a parent's natural desire to protect her child a little too far.

PLACE: Should be left vague. It will be revealed.

TIME: The present.

(Melissa enters wearing a conservative suit. She smiles warmly at the audience.)

MELISSA. Our children need to be protected, don't they? And a parent has to do whatever they can to keep their child from harm. *(Slight pause.)* D-R-U-G-S are everywhere, and I — oh, I'm sorry. My little one is here, so I have to talk in code. Just let me know if I go too fast. Anyway, D-R-U-G-S are everywhere. You see reports all the time in the news. It's going on right inside our schools. *(Slight pause.)* And that's not all. Kids are going to school with G-U-N-S and K-N-I-V-E-S. I don't know about you, but that scares the H-E-double-L out of me. *(Pause.)* I want to keep Theresa safe. She's a little girl, just four years old. Innocent. Kids should be allowed to stay that way for as long as possible. They grow up too fast these days. *(Slight pause.)* Life is hard enough. I'm sure we can all agree with that. Childhood should be a time when you don't have all those worries. I want to make sure Theresa has that time. *(Pause.)* I love my husband. Even now, I still love Kevin. Now, he thought it was time to send Theresa to school, and I know he had his reasons. School can be a valuable experience. *(Slight pause.)* But times change. School isn't the same as it was when we were children. My first day of school I was so scared about being separated from my parents and about being surrounded by kids I didn't know. Imagine how much more frightening that would be today, knowing that many of your classmates were A-R-M-E-D? *(Slight pause.)* Now, look, I'm not saying anything would happen while she was in kindergarten … of course not. *(Slight pause.)* But after that who knows? *(Slight pause.)* Will Theresa make it to third grade before she starts doing D-R-U-G-S at recess? And after D-R-U-G-S, how long will it be before she's drawn into a world of S-E-X? And S-E-X and D-R-U-G-S lead right to P-R-O-S-T-I-T-U-T-I-O-N. *(Slight pause.)* Did I spell that right? Let's see P-R-O … Well, I mean she could become a H-O-O-K-E-R. *(Pause.)* Not my little girl. *(Pause.)* I tried to convince Kevin we should keep Theresa at home and teach her ourselves. But he didn't understand, and we got into a big F-I-G-H-T. I tried to talk about it in a calm, reasonable way, but Kevin lost his T-E-M-P-E-R and Y-E L-L-E-D, and that made Theresa cry. I couldn't have let that happen. *(Slight pause.)* Ladies and gentlemen of the jury … yes, I K-I-L-L-E-D my husband. But what I did was a form of self-defense. I was protecting my daughter the way any of you would. Theresa's too young to see the world for what it is. She needs to be protected. And that is why I am innocent of M-U-R-D-E-R. *(Pause.)* Thank you. *(Melissa exits as the lights fade.)*

THE O'CONNER GIRLS

BY KATIE FORGETTE

LIZ O'CONNER — Late 40s.

SYNOPSIS: The O'Conner story takes place in 1997 in Minnesota over the Christmas holiday. Tom O'Conner has passed away, and his wife, Sarah, and their children, Liz, Martha and Matt, have reunited to excavate his mountain of personal effects. As the family sifts through boxes of papers and bags of clothing, clues to the quiet patriarch's life are discovered, prompting the usual heated arguments and some unusual revelations. As the story of Tom and Sarah's marriage unfolds, the children are forced to reconsider their long held opinions of their parents.

PLACE: Somewhere in Minnesota.

TIME: 1997 — the week after Christmas.

LIZ. Oh, no. Please! Not the "women mature faster" speech. He's fifty, Mom. Five-o. If he were any more mature we could have put him in the coffin with Dad. *(Pause.)* Sorry. *(Liz takes a cigarette out of the pack and clicks her lighter.)*
[SARAH. *Not in the house. (Liz doesn't light it but continues, undaunted.)]*
LIZ. And if Martha and I matured a little faster than he did I can tell you why. Matt woke up one day when he was twelve and discovered he had a penis —
[SARAH. *(Overlapping.) Elizabeth Louise —*
MARTHA. *(Overlapping.) Here we go …]*
LIZ. — and every time he touched it — and sometimes when he didn't — he got a feeling of euphoria rivaled only by certain narcotics. Meanwhile, at the same tender age, Martha and I discovered we were hemorrhaging — that we were in pain, retaining water, craving chocolate, and wanting to kill caring people who asked *"Is it that time?"* We had to put down dolls and check the calendar, rearrange sleep-overs, hide the necessary staunching

products — lest some tenderhearted male should see them and faint. We had to know the date, do the arithmetic and prepare, prepare, prepare. So while Matt was in the upstairs bathroom "dating" himself for hours at a time, we were doubled over in our beds with uterine contractions. *That is why women mature faster than men!* I'm going out for a smoke.

THE PAIN AND THE ITCH

BY BRUCE NORRIS

CAROL — Mother of Cash and Clay; middle-aged.

SYNOPSIS: With a young daughter in serious need of attention and a ravenous creature possibly prowling the upstairs bedrooms, what begins as an average Thanksgiving for one privileged family unravels into an exposé of disastrous choices and less-than-altruistic motives. THE PAIN AND THE ITCH is a scathing satire of the politics of class and race, a controversial, painfully human examination of denial and its consequences.

PLACE: The setting is a very nice urban home. Expensive modern decor. Not homey.

TIME: Thanksgiving evening.

CAROL. Let me ask you something. I was watching a documentary the other night on PBS. I don't know if you watch PBS. I'm a subscriber. And sometimes I volunteer for the pledge drives. But mostly I think what else is there to watch? I mean, really, well, there's the Discovery Channel. But ninety-nine percent of what's on television I just look at it and I ... I don't *disapprove,* I mean, more power to all that. Diversity and everything. Diversity is so important. But it's like with *junk food,* isn't it? I say to my first graders, if *all* you eat is junk food, then you can hardly expect to feel good about yourself. And you know, I was showing them a wonderful program all about families around the world, from each continent, and when they got to some tribesmen in New Guinea, who wear very little clothing, just some leaves and ... *gourds,* but it's the *tropics,* after all, well, some of the children started to *laugh.* And you know, that just upset me so much. So I said to them, well now, let's all just *think* for a minute. Let's think how *you* would like to be laughed at. If you went to New Guinea right now, dressed in your *American* clothes? That wouldn't be very nice, would it? How do we ever expect to reach out to new cultures and embrace new ideas if all we can do is *laugh?* *(Back to her main point.)* And plus, Bill Moyers is so wonderful. So I was watching the documentary, which was all about *Genghis Khan.* Did you see that?

PRAYING FOR RAIN

BY ROBERT LEWIS VAUGHAN

ERIN — 17.

SYNOPSIS: Marc, a high school jock suddenly stripped of his identity after a near-crippling motorcycle accident, has been adrift since the crash. His spiraling journey into self-destruction leads him into a lengthy detention with Miss K, a generous but firmly principled teacher. Although Miss K is able to make inroads with Marc, he continues his downward descent. Despite his resistance, his old friends, Jim and Chris, exert a powerful pull on him, yielding in the end staggeringly tragic results.

PLACE: The entire play takes place on The Bluffs at Dragon's Tongue, which is a red sandstone rock formation.

TIME: The past as Marc thinks about it and the present as he sees it.

ERIN. What's next, Mom? What does he have to do to make you see that he's no good? You know he still hangs out with those assholes — *(She pauses to correct her language.)* … With Jim and Chris. Maybe there wasn't a gun and they were just gonna take that kid's money. But maybe there is a gun and he'd have done it, too, I just know it, and so do you. He used to be nice and everything, I guess. He was hard to get to know. It's kinda like two Marcs: Marc before he got hurt and Marc after he got hurt. Before he got hurt, he was okay, and you'd get close enough and you'd deal with it 'cause we were all on teams, and he was kind of there, but after he got hurt … I don't know. I thought it was kind of weird, but … I mean, we all wear our team jackets, you know? Tony Miller still wears his even though he quit playing football, but. Marc always wore his jacket. He always wore it, like he was just a little more proud of it than anybody else. I noticed that after he came back to school … and he couldn't play anymore … he never wore his jacket again. And … it's like, since then, I don't know. I still … I don't want to have anything to do with him and I think they should have just kicked him out. What's he going to need a diploma for anyway? He's not going to use it.

PYRETOWN

BY JOHN BELLUSO

LOUISE — 30s.

SYNOPSIS: Louise is a divorced mother of three, getting by on welfare checks and child support in a depressed industrial New England town. Harry has been in a wheelchair since a childhood accident. Their paths cross in an emergency room as Louise seeks out care for her daughter's mysterious sickness. Yearning for connection beyond his online friends and his pile of Russian novels, Harry reaches out to help Louise navigate her daughter's care. More compatriots than lovers, they find solace with each other for a brief and intense interlude before their paths diverge.

PLACE: A New England town.

TIME: The present.

(Sound: a receptionist's voice repeating "Saint Larry's, emergency room, please hold," doctors being paged, etc. The waiting area of Saint Lawrence Hospital, emergency room. Louise is sitting near the chairs, fidgeting, waiting. Harry sits nearby in his wheelchair, flapping through the pages of a book, occasionally looking up at her. She suddenly stands.)

LOUISE. *(Speaking to a receptionist.)* No, hello, yes, no, it's not an emergency, not really. But, it is important, to me. She's, yes, I already gave you our card, yes I did, I gave it to that nurse, that one over there, with the bubble gum, yes, that's right, her. She's the one I gave it to, her, she's blowing a bubble with her bubble gum right now, yes right there. No ma'am, I definitely filled that form out already, yes I'm sure I did, no, she took both the white and the pink copies of the form, I don't have any copies at all. I'll fill out another one if you like, I don't mind, but I think the form I already filled out should be back there with our card, you see, the bubble gum lady, she fastened them all together with a paper clip, so if you can find the card … *(Short beat.)* oh good, yes, "here it is!" that's great, now if I could just say …

Yes, I'd be happy to sit back down in the chairs and continue to wait but I would first like to tell you, I, I really need to tell you; I have a large, round, wet piece of meat which is sitting on the top shelf of my refrigerator. It is called a Yankee pot roast. Yes, a Yankee pot roast which I took out of the freezer and put in the refrigerator so it would defrost. It has defrosted.

It has defrosted during these long hours that I have been sitting here waiting for a doctor to see my daughter Beatrice who has an ear infection and needs a prescription for a simple antibiotic. Yes, she's seen the triage nurse. No, the triage nurse did not diagnose her as having an ear infection, I did. I made this diagnosis because she points at her ear and says, "Owee, Owee, Owee, Mommy, Owee," to me, that means ear infection. Kids are always getting — *(Suddenly distracted, speaking to Beatrice.)* Beatrice, stop it! I mean it! Now, pick up your binky off of the floor and put it in your mouth. NOW! That's right, dust it off first, good girl. *(Back to the receptionist.)* I'm really not a cranky person, I swear I'm not, but I have two kids with me who have not had naps, I have another kid who I need to pick up from day care in … *(Looks at watch.)* seventeen minutes, and I have a Yankee pot roast which I need to cook and slice into little pieces for my kids to eat, and eventually, for me to eat as well. I am tired of waiting. I want to see a doctor, NOW!

THE RADIANT ABYSS

BY ANGUS MacLACHLAN

ERIN — 40.

SYNOPSIS: Mix the feral, native smarts of forty-year-old Erin, a sexy survivor of an abusive marriage, with the arrival of shadowy religious men of The Garden of Paradise Cultural Oasis next door to her property management office, and Erin's naturally high octane engine revs into overdrive. She seduces her former employee, twenty-three-year-old nighttime security guard Steve Enloe into roping his current girlfriend, a seemingly innocent, will-o'-the-wisp Kinko's girl, into a scheme to investigate and possibly vandalize the "so-called church," an organization that may or may not believe in violence to promote their ends.

PLACE: Winston-Salem, North Carolina.

TIME: The present.

ERIN. But I want to just say something. *(She takes a moment.)* I've seen ... Violence — Evil. In my life. Up close. I know what a dangerous man looks like. I can smell it. I know how they stare at you that second before. And then break your jaw ... Because you have your own opinion. Or your skirt's too short. Or just ... because ... And these people next door, these righteous men next door, they stink of it. *(She stops. She takes a deep breath.)* ... And I'm not standing for it. Ever again. *(Ina sees Erin struggling to keep control.)* ... You know how an animal'll gnaw off it's own leg to survive? ... At that moment of decision ... that moment turns you into someone else. You can't close your eyes anymore and look the other way. Your whole being becomes focused. Like a bolt of lightning. And you're never the same. *(She pulls back some.)* Something must be done ... But, if you two are just too young to get it — I guess — Lord love ya. If people are just too — too — STUPID to recognize till it's too late — Well, I can't help 'em. I don't even want to try!

REGRETS ONLY

BY PAUL RUDNICK

TIBBY McCULLOUGH — a lifelong Manhattan social heroine, a woman who's wanted nothing more than a fabulously interesting and expensive life. She's wonderfully poised and attractive; her hair is an extravagant ash blonde, not tacky but triumphant. She's wearing an evening gown that's both age appropriate but not at all matronly; she looks sexy and chic and might sport a few snazzy diamonds. Tibby is from a fine WASP background, but fashion is her life.

SYNOPSIS: This comedy of Manhattan manners explores the latest topics in marriage, friendships and squandered riches. The setting: a Park Avenue penthouse. The players: a powerhouse attorney, his deliriously social wife and their closest friend, one of the world's most staggeringly successful fashion designers. Add a daughter's engagement, some major gowns, the president of the United States, and stir.

PLACE: New York City.

TIME: The present.

TIBBY. Spencer, I love you very much, but first of all, I want you to stop whining and whimpering. Because the world doesn't owe you a wedding.
[SPENCER. What?]
TIBBY. And Mother, you raised me and I owe you my life, but I want you to stop treating me like a brain-damaged child.
[HANK. I'm with ya!
MYRA. Damn right!]
TIBBY. And Myra, you are going to start cleaning in the corners!
[MARIETTA. (To Myra.) It's called a Swiffer!
HANK. Bravo!]
TIBBY. And Hank, I think you've got a thing or two to learn about friendship. And respect. And destroying people's lives. So you're going to call up all of your little buddies, up and down the entire Eastern seaboard, because they're all going right back to

82

work, by tomorrow morning.

[*JACK. (To Tibby.) Thank you. Because I know that wasn't easy. And Hank, maybe now you'll finally understand something. Tibby made her choice for the very best reasons. Because I'm her husband. And we're married.*]

TIBBY. And Jack, you're going to call your new best friend, the president of the United States, and you are going to tell him that you and Spencer are off that amendment.

[*JACK. (Shocked.) Why?*]

TIBBY. Because you're right. We are married. And if that's what gay people want — let 'em learn! Because you know something? Marriage sucks. Raising a family sucks. And falling in love sucks. And you know why? Because we're all gonna die. But before I do, I wanna look gorgeous. I want hair and makeup and dresses and diamonds, I wanna make the biggest drag queen of all time say, honey, too much. I want a world that doesn't exist, that can't exist, a world where everyone's happy, where everyone's children are perfect, where everyone's mother is perfect, and where everyone's husband has fantastic sex with her, pays for everything, tells her she's beautiful, and leaves. I wanna live inside a Hank Hadley advertisement in the September issue of *Vogue*, the issue that weighs eighteen pounds because it's so packed with lies. That's what I want, and all of you, that's what you're gonna give me. Because I'm a rich white woman, and goddamnit, that's good. We're gonna make it good. And we're gonna have a wedding, because weddings are gorgeous and glorious, and that's how we trick people into getting married. So you just call the President, and you just tell him — I need flowers! I need music! And may God help me, I need cake!

A SMALL, MELODRAMATIC STORY

BY STEPHEN BELBER

O — Female, 38, odd, black, funny, harsh, sad.

SYNOPSIS: In Washington, D.C., a widow named O is trying to figure out whether life is worth reengaging with. In her path are the 1968 riots, the first Gulf War, the Freedom of Information Act and herself. There's also an archivist named Keith, a cop named Perry and a kid named Cleo. And finally, there's the question of just how much about anything do we really need to know.

PLACE: Washington, D.C.

TIME: The present.

O. *(To audience.)* Here's a cliché: lonely woman on a subway car, masturbating with the rhythm of the train's passage, the gentle movements soothing, coaxing, enlightening her very being. *(Beat.)* I bring this up — and by the way, that might not actually be a cliché, in fact, it might just be me being rather … odd — but I bring it up because it has to do with transformation. Enlightenment — emotional, intellectual, *physical* — *is* transformation. To experience *illumination* is to learn, and thus to know; to know *more. (Pause.)* And it takes so little to do this: a thought, a notion, a slight, barely perceptible *shudder:* these are *transformative* events. I *know* this. Because I used to be a transformative person.

Transformative people are people who *seek* knowledge. And then use it as means to a better end. They tend to seize the broken day; fix the unfixable, transcend the ungodly, unstick the stuck heart. Knowledge is the saber with which they slay the demon night. With knowledge they fire the skies; throw paint against walls; create chocolate angels who bring forth the Golden Rule. They're control freaks with fabulous hearts. Know-it-alls wearing coveralls as they tiptoe through the tulips. They're untouchable; unstoppable; never to be denied freedom because they've learned how to transform. *(Beat.)* And I used to be one of them. Until I tried to know too much.

SOUTHERN HOSPITALITY

BY JESSIE JONES, NICHOLAS HOPE, JAMIE WOOTEN

TWINK FUTRELLE — 40s; middle Futrelle sister.

SYNOPSIS: The Futrelle Sisters — Frankie, Twink, Honey Raye and Rhonda Lynn — are in trouble again. Their beloved hometown, Fayro, Texas, is in danger of disappearing, but Honey Raye, with a major assist from her former nemesis, Geneva Musgrave, has come up with a possible solution. A salsa manufacturing factory is looking to relocate, and a company representative is headed to Fayro on a scouting mission. Honey Raye, as the president of the Chamber of Commerce, makes promises that are not to be believed in order to woo the rep to choose Fayro. In fact, Honey Raye has told them that on the very weekend of the rep's visit, the town just happens to be having their biggest celebration of the year: "Fayro Days," which includes a craft show, a pet costume parade, a beauty pageant and a huge Civil War battle reenactment. Now the citizens of Fayro have to quickly make her promises a reality. Added to this is the dilemma of Twink being so desperate to get married that she's practically dragging the unwilling groom, Deputy John Curtis Buntner, to the altar. But how the Futrelle sisters and the other citizens of Fayro pull together and save their town is a testament to Southern strength and ingenuity.

PLACE: In and around the home of Frankie and Dub Dubberly, located in the town of Fayro, Texas.

TIME: The present.

TWINK. *(She's been pushed too far.)* Did I hear you say *forbid?* Excuse me, but who's caught fifty-three wedding bouquets in a row and has a sack full of the withered, old things to prove it? Me! Who's thrown all the bridal showers and watched everybody in the world get married and live happily ever after? Me! Who drives me home and tells me "good night" and tucks me into bed? Me! Well, you know what? I am sick and tired of being alone! Marrying John

Curtis Buntner is the end of my rainbow and I am ready, right now, today to claim my pot of gold, do you understand me? And I do not care if it harelips the governor. I'm going to get some of that happily-ever-after for myself even if I have to beat the tar out of every one of you to get you to help me do it! Today is *my* day, and if any one of you does anything to try to steal attention away from me, I swear to you, I will LOSE IT!!!

STRING FEVER

BY JACQUELYN REINGOLD

LILY — Just turned 40. Funny, smart, quirky. Looking for answers.

SYNOPSIS: In this comedy, Lily juggles the big issues: turning forty, artificial insemination and the elusive scientific Theory of Everything. Lily's world includes an Icelandic comedian, her wisecracking best friend, a cat-loving physicist, her no-longer-suicidal father and an ex-boyfriend who carries around a chair.

LILY. *(Out/in her head.)* I can't believe I am here. On this chair. With this fork, this plate, those flowers, his daylilies my forget-me-nots his smell my fear his heat you are right next to me and I could reach over and touch. I want to lock the door, I want to go inside with you and lock all the doors. *[(To him:) Good food.*
MATTHEW. Good.
LILY. It's good you kept your career going.
MATTHEW. I did my best.
LILY. Good. You still in therapy?
MATTHEW. Yup.
LILY. How's it going?
MATTHEW. It's going.]
LILY. *(Out/in her head.)* I have tried to move on it's not like I haven't tried I have. It's a mystery. I mean, it's bottomless. Makes no sense. I want to touch you so bad my hands are shaking, and I can't eat, I'm starving and well out of my mind really which makes me think there's not that much difference, you know, between us, I keep mine hidden, well so do you, but not a day goes by Matt that I don't crave you that I don't have to have you that I wouldn't stick you up my nose or in my arm, if I could only crush you into a powder, melt you in a spoon or drink you from a cup. You are in brightly lit close-up and there's nothing else and no matter how you've changed or how you really look I see the answer, I see this house, I see what I saw when we first met, even if you're frowning I see that smile those eyes that promise that said being close to you would make it better. I keep thinking

you're still him, not someone else, not one of those people you feel sorry for. And I can't put the two together.

THE STORY

BY TRACEY SCOTT WILSON

LATISHA — Teenager.

SYNOPSIS: An ambitious black newspaper reporter, Yvonne Wilson, goes against her editor, Pat Morgan, to investigate a murder and finds the BEST story ... but at what cost? Wilson explores the elusive nature of truth as the boundaries between reality and fiction, morality and ambition become dangerously blurred.

PLACE: An American city.

TIME: The present.

LATISHA. Listen, I heard you were looking for me, and I have to tell you something. First off, my name is not Latisha, and I'm really, really sorry.
[YVONNE. Sorry about what?]
LATISHA. I'm not ... I'm not in a gang. *(Pause.)* And I don't know about any murder.
[YVONNE. What? What the fuck are you talking about?]
LATISHA. I was just playing with you. I was just playing.
[YVONNE. Playing?! Are you kidding me? Playing?!]
LATISHA. You know I just ... I go to boarding school and they are fascinated by a ghetto girl like me. Fascinated. How do you get your hair like that? Have you ever seen anybody murdered? I get so sick of it. So, you know, I just make up shit to pass the time. I tell them I'm in a gang, and my mother is on crack. They think I'm supposed to be like that so I just ... My mother is a librarian. I barely leave the house when I come home from school. *(Seeing Yvonne's expression.)* Are you ... Are you alright?
[YVONNE. Why would you do this to me? Why would you? I told you about my sister, my life. I encouraged you. I helped you.]
LATISHA. You helped me? No ... I ... See ... I ... *(Pause.)* Listen, I'm sorry. I'm ... *Mi dispiace.** (Pause.)* I tell you it's hard keeping

* *I am sorry.*

90

it real sometimes. *(Pause.)* I don't know ... *(Pause.)* When I saw you that day I wondered if it would work on one of us. I mean, I could tell you were different. Not really one of us. Like me kinda. Just the way you ... I don't know. *(Pause.)* I look around my neighborhood and I wish I could move. Everybody acts so stupid. But they're not stupid. They just act stupid. You know Frantz Fanon says the oppressed are taught to believe the worst about themselves. So I just wanted to see. I spoke Italian and German to you and you still believed I was in a gang. *(Pause.)* Just like the people at school. *(Pause.)* Just like them.

SUCH A BEAUTIFUL VOICE IS SAYEDA'S

BY YUSSEF EL GUINDI

Adapted from the short stories by Salwa Bakr

SAYEDA — A wife and mother.

SYNOPSIS: SUCH A BEAUTIFUL VOICE IS SAYEDA'S transports you to another world. Here, Islam hangs in the very air you breathe; spirits, or jinns, may lurk near; flattering dresses and lipstick are evidence of infidelity; and a woman singing can bring dishonor and ruin to herself and her family.

(Sheets and clothes hang on an upstage clothesline.)

SAYEDA. Listen to me! *(She pushes him away.)* Something happened this morning and I need to tell you. Because I don't know where it came from or how to explain it. *(A final laugh — beat — then a shrug, from Abdel Hamid.)*
[*ABDEL HAMID. Sure — sure. Go ahead. I like a good joke.*]
SAYEDA. It's not a joke. It happened after you left for work, this morning. It's … I don't know where to begin … *(As Sayeda narrates what happened, Abdel Hamid will sit down to drink his tea, plopping in three or four sugar cubes.)* As soon as you left and I — I sent the children off to school … I went about my usual routine: I prepared dinner, cleaned the house and all those other household chores that never seem to end. And then when I heard the noon call to prayer I thought, why not take a bath. I deserved a break. So I did. *(Lights up on the bathtub. "Sayeda" — or Sayeda 2 — is in the tub.)* I got a bucket of water. — I washed my hair, and I, as I sometimes do, I began to sing, to amuse myself. You know how I do sometimes. But as I was singing and scrubbing myself, I experienced the strangest thing. *(Sayeda looks at Sayeda 2.)* You see — the voice that was singing … it wasn't my own. — At least it wasn't my normal voice and nothing I recognized. It was like someone else had stepped into

92

the room and was singing instead. *(Sayeda approaches the bathtub — we hear this other voice singing faintly over the speakers.)* And it was so beautiful. This voice. That felt like it might be coming out of my mouth but that wasn't mine. Well, beautiful or not, you can imagine how I reacted. I thought someone had come into the room. But when I washed the soap from my eyes and looked around — there was no one there. Everything was as it should be. — I was so scared. — I muttered a prayer to God to protect me ... and went back to cleaning myself ... And I started to sing again.

TEA

BY VELINA HASU HOUSTON

HIMIKO HAMILTON — 40s.

SYNOPSIS: Four women come together to clean the house of a fifth after her tragic suicide upsets the balance of life in their small Japanese immigrant community in the middle of the Kansas heartland. The spirit of the dead woman returns as a ghostly ringmaster to force the women to come to terms with the disquieting tension of their lives and find common ground so that she can escape from the limbo between life and death, and move on to the next world in peace — and indeed carve a pathway for their future passage.

PLACE: Junction City, Kansas, and netherworlds.

TIME: 1968.

(Himiko enters and comes downstage center. She wears a pretty, youthful kimono. A light fades up on her and a period song fades in to mark the postwar-era in Japan.)

HIMIKO. War's over. Strange-looking tall men with big noses and loud mouths are running our country. Our new supreme commander is called MacArthur, the great military savior who will preserve our ravaged nation … but who cannot preserve the common soul. *(A pause.)* Last night, coming home from a wedding, I see my mother in her best kimono walking by the river. She takes off her geta and puts her feet in the water. Her face is peaceful. So lovely, like the moon in the shadows of the clouds. She slips her small hand into the river and picks up a large stone. Looking at it for only a moment, she drops it in her kimono sleeve. Suddenly, she begins filling both sleeves with stones. I try to stop her, but she fights. The same stones I played with as a child sagging in her kimono sleeves, she jumps into the currents. I watch her sink, her long black hair swirling around her neck like a silk noose. Her white face, a fragile lily; the river, a typhoon. I wondered what it felt like to be a flower in a storm.

TEA

BY VELINA HASU HOUSTON

HIMIKO HAMILTON — 40s.

SYNOPSIS: Four women come together to clean the house of a fifth after her tragic suicide upsets the balance of life in their small Japanese immigrant community in the middle of the Kansas heartland. The spirit of the dead woman returns as a ghostly ringmaster to force the women to come to terms with the disquieting tension of their lives and find common ground so that she can escape from the limbo between life and death, and move on to the next world in peace — and indeed carve a pathway for their future passage.

PLACE: Junction City, Kansas, and netherworlds.

TIME: 1968.

HIMIKO. It's tough in Tokyo after the Yankees take our country. I have six sisters. My father screams about all the daughters my mother left him with. "Too crowded, no money." If I want a new dress, I have to work for it. There is this cabaret. My girlfriend says let's go be dancers. I think she means onstage. Like movies, dancing in pretty dresses while people watch and clap. I find out too late it means dancing with Americans. Fifty yen-a-dance. *[…]* It was simple; it was a job. "Good evening. Welcome, welcome. Fifty yen. Do you want a dance, soldier?" *(Mimics taking money and stands in surprise.)* Five hundred yen! No, no. Too much. Take it back, please. *(Offers it back.)* *[…]* His name was Billy, a cute white boy from Oklahoma. He came back every week and danced only with me. Never said too much, but he brought me flowers every time. He taught me how to do the "lindy hop" *(She begins dancing and twirls around, finally stopping full of laughter; it settles into a smile.)* … among other things. *(A pause.)* It was my first time. *(A pause.)* There was a teacher. Japanese. He taught at a university at Aoyama. He liked me. Truly. I was going to marry him. Good family. But I can't tell him I wasn't working at the trading company as an operator anymore. I can't tell him I am no longer respectable. So I just say I am sorry. I say my family won't accept the marriage. And I go back to the cabaret and wait for Billy.

tempODYSSEY

BY DAN DIETZ

GENNY — Young woman.

SYNOPSIS: "It wasn't me. It was the black hole." With these words, a temp worker named Genny launches us on an epic, fantastical journey through corporate America, Appalachia, astrophysics and beyond. TEMPODYSSEY tells the story of a young woman who's convinced she's the goddess of death. Fleeing the imminent creation of a black hole on one side of the country, she lands smack in the middle of a bomb manufacturing company on the other. Her only hope lies in the unlikely guise of a nameless temp, Dead Body Boy who considers himself immortal. Can he help Genny cast off her dark mythology once and for all? Or will she explode, taking all of downtown Seattle with her?

PLACE: A very tall office building smack in the middle of downtown Seattle.

GENNY. I know. I know about mortality. I was a chicken-choker.
  As in I grabbed chickens firmly by the neck and swung them around in a funky circumference and CRACKED THEIR NECKS. A human neck is only meant to be turned approximately ninety degrees in either direction. A chicken's is a little more flexible, it can rotate about one hundred and twenty degrees to the right or left. But very few animals have necks that can swivel three hundred and sixty degrees, and even then we're talking it's only supposed to go once. Not twice (seven hundred and twenty degrees). Thrice (one thousand and eighty degrees). Or more, more, more, more, MOOOOORRRRE! *(CRRRRRRRRRRRAAACK!!! Appalachia. Genny, her drawl creeping in from offstage to gather in the hollows of her mouth, grows younger and younger as we watch.)*
  Oh, I was gooooood. I was a little girl, no more'n eight years old, when I choked my first chicken. I'd been watching Daddy getting ready for Thanksgiving, filling orders for all the folks in town who wanted turkey but settled for chicken. He was efficient. He was quick. He was surgical in his precision. The stance: legs slightly more

than hip-width apart. Feet planted. Kind of like a baseball batter up at the plate. The grip: fingers firm, real firm, but the rest of the arm loosey-goosey. The chicken is tossed slightly in one direction, for momentum, then begins to fall in the other and is swung in a whipcrack twist and — *(CRRRRRRRRRRRRRRRRAAAACCCK!!!)*

And a shiver run updown through my spinal column. Like the ghost of that chicken electrocuted me, charged through the holes in my witnessing eyes, shrieked into my brain and surged down my spine and quivered into my legs and ZZZZZZZZZZZAAAAP!!! out my body back into the deep red mountain dirt from whence it came. Dust to dust is oversimplifying the matter. The equation is actually dust to lasergorge lightningsong howlabout hungertrick lipquiver backbanging holyriver huntrunner blacksaddle thunder-shock hiss-a-bit to dust. But where holy books are concerned, lots of stuff gets lost in translation.

I was a chicken-choker. And this is how it started. Daddy went inside to answer the telephone, take down another chicken order. And I walked on over to the cubical cage he was keeping them in. They were beating their wings, buffeting each other, there was some blood. Daddy didn't usually do this kind of thing, keep them crammed together like that, but for Thanksgiving he had to, the chickens could sense death coming on a mass scale, descending with ripple-fingers to take cold hold of each and every one of them, so the jig was definitely up and the only way to get it done was to just jam them all together in one place and reach and pull and swing and crack and reach and pull and swing and crack and *(Genny is now a little girl.)* REACH and PULL and SWING and CRACK and REACH *(Genny reaches.)* and PULL *(Genny pulls.)* and SWING *(Genny swings.)* and CRACK! *(Terrible wrenching CRRRRRRRRAAAAACCCCK!!! Genny seizes up as the rush of mortality surges through her little body. Her eyes go wide. It subsides. Genny looks down at the dead chicken in her hand. She starts to cry.)* I broke something.

I broke something.

I BROKE SOMETHING!!!

THIRD

BY WENDY WASSERSTEIN

LAURIE JAMESON — A very attractive 54-year-old woman.

SYNOPSIS: His name is Woodson Bull III, but you can call him "Third." And Professor Laurie Jameson is disinclined to like his jockish, jingoistic attitude. He is, as she puts it, "a walking red state." Believing that Third's sophisticated essay on King Lear *could not possibly have been written by such a specimen, Professor Jameson reports his plagiarism to the college's Committee of Academic Standards. But is Jameson's accusation justified? Or is she casting Third as the villain in her own struggle with her relationships, her age and the increasingly polarized political environment?*

PLACE: A small New England college.

TIME: The academic year of 2002–2003.

LAURIE. I object! I object! *King Lear* is a tragedy, not a potboiler! It can't be reduced to sublimated desire!

   Christ, it's hot in here. You'd think once you're charging people forty thousand dollars a year for tuition, they'd at least get the heating right. *(Laurie unbuttons her shirt.)* There, that's better. And by the way, why does it always come down to Daddy? "Daddy wants to keep his daughter. Daddy won't give a dowry to his daughter. Daddy wants to sleep with his daughter." I'm sure if Mr. Bull were writing his paper on this committee meeting, he would say that I wanted to sleep with him. The truth is, I have no desire to sleep with Woodson Bull. On the other hand, why do I care so much?

   If we permit this kind of unethical behavior within these gates, then inevitably it will proliferate outside them. And this man's type of easygoing insidious charm and amoral intelligence will continue to be rewarded with the most powerful positions in this country. That's why I need to be vigilant. I want to bang my fist on his head and say, "I know who you are, goddamn it! You're a walking red state!" And if I can't bang the President on the head, or the Vice-

President on the head or bang both of their heads together, why can't I hold Woodson Bull the Third accountable? *(Laurie begins to put her shirt back on.)* Ladies and gentlemen of the committee, I know there is something very wrong with the world we're living in. And the only way I can see to change things is for me to point out that Woodson Bull the Third's paper is not original. And if I can't exercise that power, then what's the point of my existence?

In conclusion, my honest feeling is, to quote *King Lear*, "Nothing can come of nothing."

TWO SISTERS AND
A PIANO

BY NILO CRUZ

SOFIA — 24, the younger sister.

SYNOPSIS: Set in 1991 during the Pan-American Games in Havana and while the Russians are pulling out of Cuba, this play portrays two sisters: Maria Celia, a novelist, and Sofia, a pianist, serving time under house arrest. Passion infiltrates politics when a lieutenant assigned to their case becomes infatuated with Maria Celia, whose novels he has been reading.

PLACE: Cuba. A spacious colonial house.

TIME: 1991.

SOFIA. I've lost a whole life of stitches in this house. A whole life. That's what gets to me. So many days, gone ... I could knit a bed-spread for this whole island with all the lost days. I can't even remember where I left off living my own life. My own place in this mess! I'll never forget that day when Papi left the country. When he kissed us on the forehead and told us not to fall in love, not to get married, because he was going to send for us ... As if love was a car one could stop with the touch of the brakes. For me time stopped. I felt my feet stop growing, my bones, my breasts, as if I had frozen in time, because I was saving myself for North America. It just feels like all my life I've been waiting and I haven't lived. You got to travel with your books. You got married, when you got tired of waiting. But me, stuck here. Stuck, piano lessons, a few students, taking care of Mamá. Stuck ... Stuck ... Stuck ... And now stuck even more.
[MARIA CELIA. Sofie please ... (Holds Sofia's arm, trying to console her.)]
SOFIA. No. Can't you see what you are doing?! Can't you see what you're getting yourself into with that man? He's not going to make

it better for us. I've watched him ... He got rid of all the inspectors who used to come to this house. He's the only one who comes here. Can't you see it spelled out on his forehead. Ownership! Everything about him screams out zookeeper.

WHITE PEOPLE

BY J.T. ROGERS

MARA LYNN DODDSON — Mid-30s.

SYNOPSIS: Now — right now — what does it mean to be a white American? What does it mean for any American to live in a country that is not the one you were promised? WHITE PEOPLE is a controversial and darkly funny play about the lives of three ordinary Americans placed under the spotlight: Martin, a Brooklyn-born high-powered attorney for a white-shoe law firm in St. Louis; Mara Lynn, a housewife and former homecoming queen in Fayetteville, NC; and Alan, a young professor struggling to find his way in New York City. Through heart-wrenching confessions, they wrestle with guilt, prejudice, and the price they and their children must pay for their actions.

PLACE: Mara Lynn's kitchen in Fayetteville, NC.

TIME: Now. Sunday.

MARA LYNN. Addison James, you get back in bed, you shut your mouth or I'm gonna whoop you like a red-headed stepchild! *(We hear the voice calling after someone again.)* All right … That's a good boy … That's right … Mama loves you. *(Mara Lynn Doddson enters her kitchen in Fayetteville, NC.)* I swear that boy is dumb as a turd. *(She wears a slightly faded dress. It is before dawn on Sunday and she has been up all night. Her hair is pulled back out of her eyes, which are worn and lined from lack of sleep.)* I mean, flesh of my flesh, but he does not listen. Dr. Singh says it's normal. Says we spoiled him; being too worried. Says all the boy needs is more discipline. Dr. Singh's full of advice. Dr. Jagdeep Singh. He's an Indian. Not one of ours, but from over there. You know: *(She points to her forehead.)* Where they wear those little red doohickeys. Earl says they look like they're renting their heads out for target practice. Earl's not especially bright.

First time I went to the hospital, all the way to Chapel Hill, I was very impressed. Everything was so big and white and sort of … hummed. This pulsing, shiny feel coming off everything. Sort of like:

"This is important. This will cost you money."

I was with Addison James in the waiting room and he was running around like a banshee. I figured, let one of these people deal with him. I mean, that's their job, right? I'm looking through the magazines. Huge stack of them piled up for our viewing pleasure. Only, see, he's got all kinds of different ones. Magazines from New York City; Paris, France. High fashion and high living. And this — this is another world. Like a strange and foreign thing. Women with shaved heads and tattoos. Women with their titties pierced. I am talking one hundred percent honest-to-God pierced. What is that about? What kind of statement are they making? Like some sort of code I don't even know. I mean, who said that was acceptable? Who went and changed the world? *(The sound of a car driving by. She stops and listens as it continues on. Then she resumes.)* Dr. Singh sits in that room where Addison James gets all hooked up and tries to explain. He's there with his legs crossed, tapping a shiny black pen on some chart, all nods and smiles. But it's just — If I'm bone-honest, he makes me tense. He talks all funny. This high-pitched voice and that accent; sorta singsongy, like a cartoon. *(Imitating Dr. Singh's voice.)* "Hello, Mrs. Doddson! And how are you today?"

I mean that is funky. All the doctors I grew up with made you feel comfortable. Had a name you could pronounce. But Dr. Jagdeep Singh — I know! He's a "specialist." But he's always using words I don't understand. He's yapping on and it's — Whoosh! Right over my head. I just have to sit there, pretend I'm following along. Scared to death he's gonna ask a question. I'm nodding, smiling. He's looking straight through me. Like I'm not even there.

Earl didn't like Dr. Singh to begin with. But, see, that's 'cause the first time, when we were there, Dr. Singh said how much he liked the name Addison James. That just drove Earl mad. See, we fought like hell when Addison James was born. Earl wanted to call him Buck. I said: *(As if talking to Earl.)* "Buck? Buck is something laying dead on the hood of your truck. Might as well just call the boy Carcass."

THE WIND CRIES MARY

BY PHILIP KAN GOTANDA

EIKO HANABI — 29.

SYNOPSIS: Loosely based on Hedda Gabler, *THE WIND CRIES MARY is set on a college campus in the late '60s. Amidst the turbulent anti-war demonstrations and beginnings of Asian-American identity politics, Eiko Hanabi, an extraordinary woman, makes her way through the course of several days, whose events will alter her life forever. Eiko finds herself caught between life choices made during a different political and racial climate, and a newer emergent model that promises more freedom and choice. Eiko is a woman caught on the cusp of a world changing from Oriental to Asian-American.*

PLACE: San Francisco.

TIME: 1968.

(Eiko enters holding a small sword-knife.)

EIKO. Some prefer pistols. Me? The *aikuchi!* My mother's mother's mother's … *[…]* Belonged to my great-grandmother. A woman can be Samurai, too. They weren't allowed to use the bigger blade, though. Always the short end. Ain't it a bitch being a girl … *(Starts to demonstrate her skill with the blade.)* "You're such a nice *otonashi* Daddy's girl" — quiet, well-behaved, subservient. "But here in America, remember, you must speak up or you're ignored." But when I open my mouth and say what I think — "Oh no, I'm a castrating American bitch." The worst of the East mixed with the worst of the West … *(She slashes.)* Better to nod and smile. I haven't the faintest idea what he's saying — nod and smile, nod and smile … You want to marry me? Nod and smile … Buy me a house? Nod and smile … Give you babies? *(Slashes violently.)* It was also used to commit *ojigi*, if you were captured by the enemy. Rather than let yourself be *defiled* by your *husband's rival*, you would kill yourself by doing thus … *(Demonstrates.)* … slashing your carotid artery

105

and bleeding to death. But before you did that — this is interesting — you'd tie your legs together, because, God forbid, when you're thrashing around on the ground with blood pouring out of your neck, you should happen to *open your legs*. How indelicate.

PERMISSIONS ACKNOWLEDGMENTS

ALMOST BLUE by Keith Reddin. Copyright © 2007, Keith Reddin. Reprinted by permission of Mary Harden, Harden-Curtis Associates, 214 West 29th Street, New York, NY 10001 on the author's behalf.

ALMOST, MAINE by John Cariani. Copyright © 2007, John Cariani. Reprinted by permission of Beth Blickers, Agency for the Performing Arts, 135 West 50th Street, 17th Floor, New York, NY 10020 on the author's behalf.

AMPHIBIANS by Billy Roche. Copyright © 2003, Billy Roche. Reprinted by permission of Emily Hickman, The Agency Ltd., 24 Pottery Lane, Holland Park, London W11 4LZ, UK on the author's behalf.

THE ARCHITECTURE OF LOSS by Julia Cho. Copyright © 2005, Julia Cho. Reprinted by permission of John Buzzetti, William Morris Endeavor Entertainment, LLC, 11 Madison Avenue, 18th floor, New York, NY 10010 on the author's behalf.

AUGUST: OSAGE COUNTY by Tracy Letts. Copyright © 2009, Tracy Letts. Reprinted by permission of Ron Gwiazda, Abrams Artists Agency, 275 Seventh Avenue, New York, NY 10001 on the author's behalf.

BE AGGRESSIVE by Annie Weisman. Copyright © 2003, Annie Weisman. Reprinted by permission of John Buzzetti, William Morris Endeavor Entertainment, LLC, 11 Madison Avenue, 18th floor, New York, NY 10010 on the author's behalf.

BEAUTIFUL CHILD by Nicky Silver. Copyright © 2004, Nicky Silver. Reprinted by permission of John Buzzetti, William Morris Endeavor Entertainment, LLC, 11 Madison Avenue, 18th floor, New York, NY 10010 on the author's behalf.

BEAUTY ON THE VINE by Zak Berkman. Copyright © 2008, Zak Berkman. Reprinted by permission of Olivier Sultan, Creative Artists Agency, 405 Lexington Avenue, New York, NY 10174 on the author's behalf.

BHUTAN by Daisy Foote. Copyright © 2007, Daisy Foote. Reprinted by permission of Beth Blickers, Agency for the Performing Arts, 135 West 50th Street, 17th Floor, New York, NY 10020 on the author's behalf.

A BICYCLE COUNTRY by Nilo Cruz. Copyright © 2004, Nilo Cruz. Reprinted by permission of Peregrine Whittlesey, Peregrine Whittlesey Agency, 279 Central Park West, New York, NY 10024 on the author's behalf.

BLACK SHEEP by Lee Blessing. Copyright © 2003, Lee Blessing. Reprinted by permission of Judy Boals, Judy Boals, Inc., 262 West 38th Street, #1207, New York, NY 10018 on the author's behalf.

NOTES
(Use this space to make notes for your production)